LIFE
LESSONS
FROM WINNIE-THE-POOH

DEDICATION

In particular the Sevenoaks Pooh Posse
(Susanne, Andrew, Daniel, Simon, Big Teds, Cuthy, Dobbs and Reggie)
and anyone who has ever been (all) At Sea.

Especially Emily Morgan *and all who gibe*
in her along Life's rugged North Shore.

Namely: Anna, Ian, Imogen, Kathy, Andrew, Jonelle,
David, the Apostolic nuns, the Dixie Chicks
and Captain Richard Oswald.

*Tigger took a large mouthful of honey . . . and he looked up at the ceiling with his head on one side, and made exploring noises with his tongue, and considering noises, and what-have-we-got-*here *noises . . . and then he said in a very decided voice: 'Tiggers don't like honey.'*

THE HOUSE AT POOH CORNER

Life Lessons from Winnie-the-Pooh is about trying to make sense of life, and that means trying things out – just as Tigger did when he came to live in the Forest. When Tigger set out on his journey through the Hundred Acre Wood he had little idea of what he liked, who he was and how he fitted into the Great Scheme of Things.

With guidance from Pooh and his new friends, Tigger learnt how to live alongside others without hooshing and jostling them too much and how to channel his great zest for life into helping others, notably Baby Roo. And, of course, he discovered that Tiggers like Extract of Malt.

Life Lessons from Winnie-the-Pooh is about shedding a little light on your own path of discovery. With inspiration from Pooh and his friends it will enable you to take steps to change your life for the better. You will also find calm and tranquillity in the Hundred Acre Wood when you need it.

First published 2004
by Egmont Books Limited
239 Kensington High Street, London W8 6SA

Copyright in the compilation and commentary © 2004 Janette Marshall
The moral rights of the author have been asserted

Texts by A. A. Milne and line illustrations by E. H. Shepard from
Winnie-the-Pooh, The House at Pooh Corner, When We Were Very Young and
Now We Are Six copyright under the Berne convention.
Colouring of the illustrations from *Winnie-the-Pooh* and *The House at Pooh Corner*
copyright © 1970, 1973, 1974 E. H. Shepard and Egmont Books Limited
Colouring of the illustrations from *Now We Are Six* and *When We Were Very Young*
by Mark Burgess copyright © 1989 Egmont Books Limited

ISBN 1 4052 1203 9
3 5 7 9 10 8 6 4 2

A CIP catalogue record for this title is available
from the British Library

Book design by DickiDot Ltd

Printed and bound in Singapore

LIFE
LESSONS

FROM WINNIE-THE-POOH

JANETTE MARSHALL

EGMONT

ACKNOWLEDGEMENTS

*Winnie-the-Pooh and anyone else
who has ever had a Grand Idea.*

*Susanne Beard, Linda Coffey,
Leah Thaxton and Beth Wyllyams.*

INTRODUCTION

If you ever feel stressed by modern life, learn from the values and behaviour of Pooh and his friends. Without knowing it, they are a living example of how to achieve well-being. Between them they have a holistic approach to living, taking care of mind, body and spirit. Of course, they don't know that, because it's just the way they are. They 'get on with life' in an intuitive way, caring for themselves and each other, and they avoid intellectualising.

Yes, on the whole, Pooh and his friends are practical and caring. And so is this book. It offers you comfort and wisdom, along with . . .

- Practical solutions to everyday situations, and simple observations that might throw new light on what has been puzzling you.

- The opportunity to discover – or rediscover – what really matters in your life.

- Ways of making changes, or thinking about making changes to your life.

- A sense of purpose that might be lacking, or may have been buried in your busy life.

- The encouragement to daydream to boost your creativity and help solve problems.

- 'Permission' to 'muck about' and not feel guilty or stupid for doing so. Mucking about will probably make you happier and enrich you.

- The daring to be more spontaneous and to enjoy the moment. (How often do you miss things now because you are too busy thinking of the future or worrying about the past?)

What is well-being?

People with a sense of well-being enjoy a happier, healthier and longer life; they feel positive about themselves. But what creates that feeling of well-being?

Some people put it down to having achieved the right balance between work and the other areas of their life; some to the added buzz and energy they feel from being fitter. For some people it's more about feeling at peace with themselves, which they derive from an element of spirituality in their lives.

Whatever well-being is to you, one thing's certain: you can't go out and buy it. No matter how much money you have, it won't guarantee you health and happiness – the foundations of most people's sense of well-being.

. . . And where can you find it?

You can find well-being by learning from Pooh and his friends. But as with all of the world's greatest teachers, Pooh will raise as many questions as he answers. And that too is a Grand Thing because it may help you question what you have been doing so far with your life. So, as well as finding much comfort in the books of Pooh, you will also find some challenges that may lead you outside your comfort zone.

But be reassured you can always return to the Hundred Acre Wood, and wherever in the world your quests take you, like Christopher Robin, you can travel with the comforting thought that Pooh is always at the Top of the Forest to be consulted on any matter you please.

1 | DON'T LET FACTORS, LOGARITHMS AND ALGORITHMS KEEP YOU AWAY FROM THE HUNDRED ACRE WOOD FOR TOO LONG

Then, suddenly again, Christopher Robin, who was still looking at the world with his chin in his hands, called out 'Pooh!'
'Yes?' said Pooh.
'When I'm – when – Pooh!'
'Yes, Christopher Robin?'
'I'm not going to do Nothing any more.'
'Never again?'
'Well, not so much. They don't let you.'

THE HOUSE AT POOH CORNER

THERE COMES A point in our lives when we have to say goodbye to childhood and go out into the adult world, a world full of 'musts' and 'shoulds' and 'oughts' and 'responsibilities' and a startling lack of fun.

Living life in a way that fulfils our responsibilities, and with humour and fun, is challenging. But with so much pressure to achieve and so little time to oneself it may seem that the joy of Doing Nothing is in danger of being lost forever.

It need not be like that. You can continue to benefit from the carefree feeling and total relaxation of long, sunny summer school holidays if you stay in touch with the things you knew instinctively as a child. Then you knew when you had to stop and rest, you had a strong sense of right and wrong and a desire for fairness and justice. You could apply yourself to learning new skills and subjects and you had a sense of discovery and wonder at seeing and learning those things for the first time. You were devoid of cynicism, sarcasm and nastiness – adult attributes that are difficult to avoid absorbing after being around jaded grown-ups.

Try to keep the adult world and your problems in perspective. Come back to the Hundred Acre Wood every now and again to restore your sense of well-being. Lie on the grass, look up at the clouds scudding by or out at the world, and enjoy doing Absolutely Nothing once in a while. It's good for you.

'He's out,' said Pooh sadly. 'That's what it is. He's not in. I shall have to go a Fast Thinking Walk by myself. Bother!' . . . and while he waited for Piglet not to answer, he jumped up and down to keep warm, and a hum came suddenly into his head . . .

THE HOUSE AT POOH CORNER

FACED WITH A blank computer screen or a blank piece of paper, it's likely that your mind will also go blank. Sometimes you just can't get started. Or maybe you do get off to a good start, but after a while you get stuck. Then there are the times when your otherwise reliable partner or colleague is not around for you to bounce ideas off.

At times like these, when you simply can't order your thoughts, it is a good idea to go for a Fast Thinking Walk. Physical activity has the effect of jolting the brain into action, and even a short walk every day has been shown to improve the memory and the ability to do other mental tasks, such as planning and organising, along with making improvements to fitness.

Taking a break for physical activity can increase productivity when you return to the task in hand. It seems unlikely, but it's true: stop thinking about the problem for a while and the solution pops up of its own accord.

So don't stare at a blank screen or a blank sheet of paper for too long – take a break for a Fast Thinking Walk. And don't forget to take a small pocket notebook or tape recorder so that you can jot down the ideas as they come to you.

Edward Bear, known to his friends as Winnie-the-Pooh, or Pooh for short, was walking through the Forest one day, humming proudly to himself.

WINNIE-THE-POOH

POOH AND HIS friends enjoy many different types of walk. We have just experienced the Fast Thinking Walk that produces Grand Ideas and in the next lesson we will go on a Bonding Walk with friends. Both are different from the purposeful walks Pooh takes for visiting and the meandering, bouncy type of exercise walk preferred by Tigger, who is a veritable coiled spring of energy.

Tigger is in the minority when it comes to brisk walking, a minority both inside the Forest and outside. Only a quarter of men and women in the UK meet the recommended daily minimum of thirty minutes or more of moderate activity. Without that level of activity we put ourselves at greater risk of heart disease, type two diabetes, high blood pressure, osteoporosis and certain cancers.

Walking is an ideal form of exercise, whether you have had heart bypass surgery or have nothing wrong with you but have just got out of the habit of exercise. The idea is to warm up the muscles slowly when you begin exercise, so start any walking session at a slowish pace for about five minutes to increase circulation and breathing. After that the speed at which you walk determines how many calories you burn and the degree to which your fitness will improve. Interestingly, the heavier you are the more calories you use per minute on your walks, so Pooh burns more calories than Piglet, whether they stroll or stride. This is a particularly comforting thought for the stouter among us.

Walkers are more successful at losing weight if they walk longer distances at comfortable speeds. This kind of exercise burns off fat but is not intense enough to improve your level of fitness.

To achieve the Tigger Effect (to improve cardiovascular or heart and lung fitness) you need to work at a higher intensity, so a brisker walk, or a jog, is needed. Jogging, however, is obviously less sociable because it makes you rather breathless and sweaty and less able to discuss philosophical questions on the nature of the Universe or what's for tea.

To combine weight loss and cardiovascular conditioning, alternate Pooh Walking with Tigger Bouncing. In other words, push yourself harder on alternate days so you have one higher intensity brisk walking day (maybe even jogging) followed by a lower intensity walking day to burn fat (without burning you out).

At first as they stumped along the path which edged the Hundred Acre Wood, they didn't say much to each other; but when they came to the stream, and had helped each other across the stepping stones, and were able to walk side by side again over the heather, they began to talk in a friendly way about this and that, and Piglet said, 'If you see what I mean, Pooh,' and Pooh said, 'It's just what I think myself, Piglet,' and Piglet said, 'But on the other hand, Pooh, we must remember,' and Pooh said, 'Quite true, Piglet, although I had forgotten it for the moment.'

WINNIE-THE-POOH

WALKING HAS A way of bonding people, particularly long discursive walks. Ambling along, just chatting of this and that, preferably with a pleasant view to distract you during the comfortable silences that good companionship allows, enables you to become better acquainted with another person. Walking is a bonding activity for Pooh, Piglet and Christopher Robin. They are not the first and neither will they be the last to discover the joy of a pleasant walk and a pleasant talk. Going on such a walk is a good excuse, if one were needed, for just being with your friends. Find time to try it for yourself.

Half-way between Pooh's house and Piglet's house was a Thoughtful Spot where they met sometimes when they had decided to go and see each other, and as it was warm and out of the wind they would sit down there for a little and wonder what they would do now that they had seen each other.

The House at Pooh Corner

EVERYONE NEEDS A retreat, a quiet place. As a child your Thoughtful Spot was probably under the blankets or duvet, or in those moments between sleep and waking when you lay daydreaming, peacefully working out the world. Or perhaps you had a special den or a tree house.

Adults need their own space in which to retreat. It probably won't be under the kitchen table or constructed from cushions from the sofa. But perhaps all that is needed is a lockable desk or cupboard or maybe a special chair, perhaps behind a screen, where you can't be seen.

It's important to have some time away from the background 'noise' of everyday life, problems at work or stresses at home, to think through What To Do Next or daydream for a while. It may be that you can only find time to retreat on a specific night of the week or during part of the weekend. On some occasions it might be nice to invite someone to join you so that you can both retreat from the world for a while to recharge your batteries.

*'No Give and Take,' Eeyore went on . . .
'It's your fault, Eeyore. You've never been
to see any of us. You just stay here in this
one corner of the Forest waiting for the
others to come to you. Why don't you go
to them sometimes?'
Eeyore was silent for a little while, thinking.
'There may be something in what you say,
Rabbit,' he said at last. 'I have been
neglecting you. I must move about more.
I must come and go.'*

THE HOUSE AT POOH CORNER

YOU CAN'T (ALWAYS) blame others if you feel left out or lonely or rather Eeyore-ish and gloomy. If your social life is a bit 'rusty' maybe it's time you took the initiative. Perhaps you have been busy putting time into building your career, or saving money to buy something special, or maybe you are not happy with the way you look, or lack confidence because you don't feel as successful as you would like. There are many reasons why we avoid social situations and why the balance of life can become skewed so that we end up feeling there is something missing.

As Rabbit bluntly points out to Eeyore, sometimes it's up to you to make the first move to stop yourself feeling isolated.

If people think you are busy, or saving money, or happy in your self-contained world then they might not like to call you. You are going to have to make the first move. Call and invite friends back to your home or arrange to meet them at a bar, the cinema, bowling, theatre – wherever. If you could benefit from more exercise, try to join a gym or a sports (tennis, riding, hockey, dance, yoga) club. Maybe a dance club would suit you – anything from ballroom to salsa, and you do not have to take a partner in order to go. If you have a pleasant home with space ask people round at the weekend for drinks, lunch, a barbecue or supper – they can bring a course or make a contribution. Be interested in what other people are doing, ask them about their lives – and remember the details for the next time you meet them.

Socialising is a habit like any other, so take the initiative and assume the best. Believe that people will want to hear from you and spend time with you. The more socialising you do the more confident you will become.

ORDER OF LOOKING FOR THINGS.

1. Special Place. *(To find Piglet.)*

2. Piglet. *(To find who Small is.)*

3. Small. *(To find Small.)*

4. Rabbit. *(To tell him I've found Small.)*

5. Small Again. *(To tell him I've found Rabbit.)*

THE HOUSE AT POOH CORNER

THE SIMPLE ACT of writing To Do lists can clear the mind because you no longer have to remember the tasks once they are written down. As long as you do not allow the lists to tyrannise you, they will be helpful rather than oppressive.

Naturally, Pooh does this intuitively without having ever read a manual or attended a course on the subject of time management. The list above is one that Pooh wrote in his head when Rabbit was organising a search for Small, one of Rabbit's myriad of relatives.

Even with his innate ability to organise himself (although Pooh would not like to think of himself as Being Organised), Pooh acknowledges that having a lot of things to do 'makes it look like a bothering sort of day'.

With any To Do list, first list the tasks. Then put them in order of importance or urgency and work through them in a methodical way. Although having said that, it is always nice to put a small achievable task (and a fun one) at the top because crossing it off can spur you on to doing the more challenging ones. Some of the harder tasks might benefit from being further broken down into steps, such as Rabbit's 'Plan to Capture Baby Roo' in *Winnie-the-Pooh*.

Lists also present you with the opportunity to see where you might delegate part of the task to others – and at the same time keep a track of who is doing what, all of which transforms a bothering sort of day into a Do-able day that positively hums along.

'And that will Upset him. Because when you say "Ho-ho!" twice, in a gloating sort of way, and the other person only hums, you suddenly find, just as you begin to say it the third time that – well, you find –'

THE HOUSE AT POOH CORNER

POOH IS A peacemaker. He is a master at avoiding confrontation. If he was a bird (which he is patently not, but for argument's sake we will persist), he would be a Dove, not a Hawk, and as such he is a Great Comfort to Piglet.

Piglet is prone to hysteria, particularly when facing the prospect of capture by a Heffalump. At one point, Piglet and Pooh fall into what they assume to be a Heffalump Trap. Piglet imagines the terrible 'Ho-ho!' of the Heffalump as it confronts them, and wonders what to say to the Hostile Animal. Pooh recognises that there is nothing effective one can say to an Angry Heffalump (or an 'angry' person, come to that) so says he will not reply, he will just hum to himself.

It's Piglet who finds the words to describe what you find.

. . . it isn't ho-ho-ish any more.

Exactly. And as Pooh has demonstrated, the situation with the Heffalump has been defused without resorting to shouting, screaming or violent resistance – by far the preferable route to disarmament.

'Well, I've got an idea,' said Rabbit, 'and here it is. We take Tigger for a long explore, somewhere where he's never been, and we lose him there, and next morning we find him again, and – mark my words – he'll be a different Tigger altogether.'
'Why?' said Pooh.
'Because he'll be a Humble Tigger . . . a Sad Tigger, a Melancholy Tigger, a Small and Sorry Tigger . . . '
'I should hate him to go on being Sad,' said Piglet, doubtfully.
'Tiggers never go on being Sad,' explained Rabbit. 'They get over it with Astonishing Rapidity . . . '

THE HOUSE AT POOH CORNER

POOH AND PIGLET, and we, The Readers, are left feeling very uncomfortable about making Tigger feel small and sorry. Teaching others a lesson may seem like a good idea at the time, but would we like it to happen to us?

It is far easier to observe faults in others than to see and correct them in ourselves. In the case of Tigger, smaller animals such as Piglet want him to be less bouncy because Big Bounces are frightening. Similarly, those with a quieter disposition, such as Eeyore, find Tigger's loudness alarming.

But does feeling annoyed with someone justify teaching them a lesson? Was Rabbit right to take matters into his own hands?

Some might say Rabbit would do better to improve his own attitude to others – by learning not to be so overbearing, patronising and bossy. Perhaps he should have asked himself whether he would want to be treated as he treated Tigger. As it happened, Poetic Justice prevailed: it was Rabbit who became lost in the mist and Rabbit who ended up feeling melancholy, small and sorry.

The fact that it was Tigger who rescued Rabbit can teach us something else too . . . sometimes the very people who we find so difficult are the ones who are able to help us when we are really in need.

'There's Pooh,' he [Piglet] *thought to himself. 'Pooh hasn't much Brain, but he never comes to any harm. He does silly things and they turn out right.'*

WINNIE-THE-POOH

POOH AND PIGLET'S relationship is based on intuitive behaviour. Pooh is governed by instinct rather than intellect. He just knows what is the right thing to do to support his friends and help everyone in the Forest. He doesn't think too much, he just trusts his intuition, gets on and offers help.

Winnie-the-Pooh remains true to his instincts – unlike Christopher Robin, who has to leave the Forest to go to school, where he is taught how to override his instinctive behaviour and to conform to rules, regulations and, later in life, the restrictions of work.

And yet Christopher Robin could, and does, learn much from Pooh: there is always a place for intuition and instinct among the necessary rules and regulations of adult life. Successful managers attribute a great deal of their success to acting on intuition or gut feeling. And entrepreneurs around the world confirm that the pivotal decisions they make are a combination of analysis and intuition.

So, while intellect, good spelling and brain power are to be valued in and by those who have them, the most powerful combination, and the one which probably produces the most humane solutions, is that which counterbalances cleverness with intuition.

. . . she [Kanga] knew at once that, however big Tigger seemed to be, he wanted as much kindness as Roo . . .

THE HOUSE AT POOH CORNER

NO ONE IS ever too big or too old to have kindness shown to them. There are many ways to show kindness, from the traditional offer of seats on public transport and opening of doors, to checking if anyone is behind you before letting a door shut, and remembering to look in on elderly neighbours, or find time for a brief chat with them. And if you feel happy share it by smiling – even the strangers you pass will feel better for it.

If you have a friend who is in trouble or ill, don't just say, 'Let me know if there is anything I can do.' Make specific offers of practical help. It is then easier for them to accept a hand.

You can also show kindness by *not* doing things. If you are thinking unkind thoughts about someone, don't voice them, and resist the impulse to tell third parties gossip about someone you do not like. If you are tempted to make a witty sarcastic riposte that will make another person look stupid, then don't do it. It might make you look clever, but how does it make the recipient feel? If they are a child or inexperienced or lacking in confidence it is likely to harm them.

Bear in mind the maxim – 'If you don't have anything nice to say, don't say anything.'

'Oh Bear!' said Christopher Robin. 'How I do love you!'
'So do I,' said Pooh.

WINNIE-THE-POOH

IS POOH SAYING, in his own way, that he loves Christopher Robin, or is he saying that he loves himself? Probably both. We can speculate and analyse, but to what end when the message is clear? It's love that counts. And if you love yourself, or at least come to terms with your shortcomings and become a little more comfortable in your own skin, then you will be more confident and easier for others to be with.

There's another side to love, too. You can love and hate the same person – a common experience in families where closeness can lead to conflict and where there is sometimes a limited amount of love to go around. Which means loving is also about learning to forgive and making the effort to do better next time.

Try not to be too self-critical, or critical of your partner and family. If you are, do it constructively rather than as a form of punishment and blame, whether of yourself or others. Instead of persisting in any negative attitude you might have towards yourself, give yourself praise where it is due. Accept your failings (and the failings of others) and work to improve them. Celebrate your attributes and learn to accept compliments gracefully.

Then Piglet saw what a Foolish Piglet he had been, and he was so ashamed of himself that he ran straight off home and went to bed with a headache.

WINNIE-THE-POOH

PIGLET FELT ASHAMED because a Heffalump (that was in reality Pooh with his head stuck in a honey pot) had frightened him. Nothing to be ashamed of, you might think, and possibly more a case of embarrassment than shame. But there are more understandable reasons for feeling ashamed. For example, when we have found something and kept it without trying to find its rightful owner, or let a shop assistant give us more change than we know we are due. Even more shameful is turning the disadvantage of others to our own advantage – perhaps paying a low price for something we know to be valuable when the vendor has more need of the money than we do. And you may also have felt ashamed by the confessions of others to deeds that you have done or been tempted to do.

If we cut ourselves off from such feelings or place less importance on shame than on our own self-confidence, then we become morally worse off.

14 | APPLY SOME PLANNING AND FORETHOUGHT BEFORE YOU LICK THE JAR

'. . . I would get to the Jar of Honey, and I should lick round the edges first of all, pretending that there wasn't any more, you know, and then I should walk away and think about it a little, and then I should come back and start licking in the middle of the jar, and then –'

WINNIE-THE-POOH

LIKE POOH REHEARSING how he would enjoy a jar of honey, you too can rehearse the everyday to help your life run more smoothly, and to achieve the outcome you want. How do you do it?

For example, before you go into a business meeting, or make one of those dreaded telephone calls to a utility or services company, or attend a financial meeting (with your bank, building society or insurance broker), or make a call to your GP's surgery for an appointment or test results, write a checklist and keep it by you. List the information you need – and tick off the questions as you work through. Don't be flustered, go at the pace that suits you, and ask the person to repeat the information or advice until you feel you understand it.

Not all situations are as easy to script, however. Difficult situations at work or in the family need a lot of forethought, and often rely on immaculate timing. It is very important to choose a time when the other person is likely to be most receptive, even if that means you have to be extremely patient and put off the encounter. Put yourself in the other person's place and try to think through how they might react, what they might say and how you will deal with a variety of responses to reach a satisfactory conclusion for both sides.

But be aware that even the best-rehearsed play or event does not always go exactly to plan.

15 | WHEN COUNTING HEFFALUMPS
no longer sends you to sleep

But he [Pooh] couldn't sleep. The more he tried to sleep, the more he couldn't. He tried Counting Sheep, which is sometimes a good way of getting to sleep, and, as that was no good, he tried counting Heffalumps. And that was worse. Because every Heffalump that he counted was making straight for a pot of Pooh's honey, and eating it all. *For some minutes he lay there miserably, but when the five hundred and eighty-seventh Heffalump was licking its jaws, and saying to itself, 'Very good honey this, I don't know when I've tasted better,' Pooh could bear it no longer.*

WINNIE-THE-POOH

POOH'S INABILITY TO sleep is obviously due to anxiety about his and Piglet's Heffalump trap that they plan to visit very early the next morning. But what happens if the problem is more long-term?

When you are over-busy and experiencing constant stress at work and home these sleepless episodes can become more frequent. To prevent you feeling frazzled it's helpful to have a few Good Sleep Tactics under your pillow.

- Have the same amount of sleep each night.
- Work back from the time you need to be up in the morning.
- Make sure the bed is comfortable.
- Have a regular bedtime routine.
- Don't exercise too close to bedtime.

- Avoid heavy meals at night and caffeine and alcohol and too much TV before bed.
- Find time for regular exercise and relaxation and fresh air.
- Wear an eye mask and earplugs if necessary.
- Keep warm in bed – even consider bed socks (but have a window open).
- Don't have hot baths up to an hour before bed.
- Take a good book to bed, one that will take your mind off any worries.

Why is all this so important? Sleep is vital for the brain, especially for memory, creative and flexible thinking, concentration and working through distractions. Tests depriving people of sleep show it reduces their vocabulary, makes them less articulate, and reduces their ability to understand quickly changing situations.

If sleeplessness lasts for more than a few nights it becomes insomnia (the inability to sleep). And most cases are related to concerns about Heffalumps – in other words they are symptoms of an underlying stress (caused by anxiety or depression) which needs to be dealt with to cure the insomnia. Pain can keep you awake and if that's the case you also need help from your doctor.

The trouble is that anxiety, depression – or even worries about planning a major event – may continue for some time, during which sleep problems become habitual. So (re)establishing good sleep patterns as soon as possible is essential.

. . . 'Eeyore, who is a friend of mine, has lost his tail. And he's Moping about it. So could you very kindly tell me how to find it for him?'

'Well,' said Owl, 'the customary procedure in such cases is as follows.'

'What does Crustimoney Proseedcake mean?' said Pooh. 'For I am a Bear of Very Little Brain, and long words Bother me.'

'It means the Thing to Do.'

'As long as it means that, I don't mind,' said Pooh humbly.

WINNIE-THE-POOH

IF YOU DON'T ask you will never find out, but sometimes it is hard to admit that you don't know something, especially if other people all seem to know, or give the impression that they think you should. But we can't all be aficionados of everything and every expert has to be initiated, or let in on the secret, at some time.

For example, if you are an aged High Court judge you might not be familiar with who's who on the university band circuit and, equally, if you are a student you are unlikely to be familiar with who is likely to be appointed a Queen's Counsel this year.

We might laugh about the 'ignorance' of others when their expertise or interests do not coincide with popular (or our own) culture, but we should really respect those people who have the courage to ask questions. So take your courage in both hands and ask for an explanation or two. It is perfectly acceptable to 'show your ignorance'.

And he [Christopher Robin]
*took a stick and touched Pooh
on the shoulder, and said, 'Rise,
Sir Pooh de Bear, most faithful
of all my Knights'.*

THE HOUSE AT POOH CORNER

VERY FEW PEOPLE receive a knighthood but there are other ways to recognise and acknowledge effort – even if it is 'only' service to your family rather than the nation. Start in the home by giving praise where it is due. Thank your partner for washing up and taking out the rubbish.

Recognise the personal achievements of your friends, whether it is success at work, or making the effort to enter a fun run or a sponsored bike ride, or reaching a personal goal, such as losing weight. Praise or admire them by talking about what they have done and how they did it.

At work, thank your colleagues for support or for cover when you were on holiday or off sick. Tell them how much you appreciate their efforts, or perhaps any special talent or characteristic they bring to the workplace.

If you have contact with children, praise them for their efforts at school or in their hobbies and sports and, where appropriate, give them small gifts such as a special pencil or piece of stationery. Rewards reinforce desirable behaviour in all walks of life and they may act also as an example to those who see what is being rewarded and realise that they are not pulling their weight or making a good enough contribution.

Some employers take the opposite approach and have a 'name and shame' policy. Some supermarkets chains, for example, periodically circulate the names of managers and staff at their lowest-performing branches to shame them into working harder. This is odd because de-motivational approaches tend not to work. It is far better to recognise and reward achievement and effort to encourage better performance.

Suggest your workplace has a recognition scheme, perhaps a choice of reward twice a year for the people who contribute the most to creating a pleasant and effective working environment.

'Now,' said Rabbit, 'this is a Search, and I've Organized it –'

'Done what to it?' said Pooh.

'Organized it. Which means – well, it's what you do to a Search, when you don't all look in the same place at once. So I want you, Pooh, to search by the Six Pine Trees first, and then work your way towards Owl's House, and look out for me there. Do you see?'

'No', said Pooh. 'What –'

'Then I'll see you at Owl's House in about an hour's time.'

'Is Piglet organdized too?'

'We all are,' said Rabbit . . .

THE HOUSE AT POOH CORNER

SOME PEOPLE HAVE life coaches, some people use their partners, some rely on their personal assistants. Others, including Pooh, stoically endure Being Organised by individuals like Rabbit telling them to Keep to the Left or Sign Here or Vote for a Resolution. However, for most of us, improving our organisational skills is a question of learning how to do it for ourselves.

The main benefit of organising your time is that it reduces stress. Try thinking ahead a week at a time. Sunday night is a good time to check or plan the home diary for the coming week – liaise with your flatmate, partner, child, au pair and anyone else in the family or household that you share responsibility for or with. Monday is the obvious day to co-ordinate efforts for the week at work. Write down appointments, telephone calls to make and specific tasks for each day. You can use a calendar or sheets of paper but a diary is best, if possible, because lists can be lost and you do not carry calendars around. (Although it is very handy to have a calendar near the telephone at home.)

Putting everything in one diary (that includes work and social life) is a good way not to forget anything. Try to look at the diary each evening.

Lay out the clothes you need for the next day, pack any bags required for work and so on the night before, then if anything is missing you have some time to find it, wash it or mend it!

In addition to your work tasks make sure you write in each week some exercise or 'fun' time for yourself. Some people find it useful to pin a weekly list by the front door mentioning activities for each day. Others like to have a magnetic shopping list on the fridge door, or a chalkboard or a memo pad elsewhere in the kitchen, to list food, laundry and other items needed as they run out. Apply these tips to the relevant areas of your life and have a look at Lesson 7, which is about prioritisation.

One day Rabbit and Piglet were sitting outside Pooh's front door listening to Rabbit, and Pooh was sitting with them. It was a drowsy summer afternoon, and the Forest was full of gentle sounds, which all seemed to be saying to Pooh, 'Don't listen to Rabbit, listen to me.' So he got into a comfortable position for not listening to Rabbit, and from time to time he opened his eyes to say 'Ah!' and then closed them again . . .

After a while, Piglet nudges Pooh as Rabbit has become aware that Pooh is not listening . . .

. . . and Pooh, who felt more and more that he was somewhere else, got up slowly and began to look for himself.

THE HOUSE AT POOH CORNER

IN THIS BUSY life, it is vital to find time to still the mind and enjoy some peace and quiet or listen to nature – the buzz of bees on a warm day, the twitter of birds and the rustle of leaves in a breeze, or the invigorating rush of the wind on a blustery winter morning. Listening to these natural sounds can help hush the constant babble and turmoil of the inner voice in your head or, in Pooh's case, the incessant burbling of Rabbit.

The intermittent, quiet sounds of nature are soothing and restorative, unlike the ugly noise of traffic and the intrusive urban racket of loud radios, pneumatic drills and electric lawn mowers. Just a short outdoor walk at lunchtime can reinvigorate you, especially if it removes you from the chatter of over-talkative colleagues in open-plan offices or of friends and family at home.

We all need time to listen to the bees, hear the birds sing and drift away. Try lying on your back in the garden or park watching clouds scudding high in the sky, or listen to the rhythmic drift and drag of pebbles on a beach as the waves lap the shore.

Once you discover your favourite sounds of nature you can fix them in your mind so that you can retreat there whenever you need to relax, or when you can't sleep. Let yourself go and surrender to that semi-hypnotic trance-like state that seems peculiar to still summer days, the feeling that Pooh was enjoying before one of Rabbit's questions required him to stir and bring his mind back to earth.

And a Help-yourself with Rabbit
Though it may become a habit,
Is a pleasant sort of habit
For a Pooh.

THE HOUSE AT POOH CORNER

POOH IS A habitual snacker. At about eleven o'clock each morning he has a little something, whether he is hungry or not (but, of course, he always is). And we would not want him to change, but we might want to change our own behaviour by observing the effect that habitual over-eating has on his girth. Pooh starts the day with breakfast, followed by elevenses, then lunch, then very nearly tea and then tea – only Hobbits eat more!

Small changes do make a difference. By eating one less biscuit a day, or one less teaspoonful of honey, or walking a mile a day, we can 'save' around 100 calories a day. It doesn't sound much but over time it adds up to enough to prevent the average two pounds or one kilogram weight gain that most adults put on each year of their adult life.

Sticking to three meals a day, and limited snacks, will help prevent weight gain and health problems. Snacking in front of the TV, for example, adds the equivalent of an extra meal a day to many people's food intake. That adds up to a lot of extra calories in a short time.

As a rough guide, eat at least five portions of fruit and vegetables a day, six to eleven (depending on age, sex and activity level) portions of wholegrain or starchy foods such as bread (wholemeal bread is particularly delicious with honey – no need to add spread), rice, pasta or potatoes. And two to three portions of low-fat dairy (yoghurt, milk, cheese) and low-fat protein foods (fish, meat and vegetarian alternatives).

In addition, step up your activity level. Take your lead from Pooh, who frequently has a brisk stomp through the Forest before lunch or as a prelude to taking tea with Owl or Rabbit. And if you eat more, move more.

'I'm planting a haycorn, Pooh, so that it can grow up into an oak-tree, and have lots of haycorns just outside the front door instead of having to walk miles and miles, do you see, Pooh?'

THE HOUSE AT POOH CORNER

PIGLET'S MOTIVES MIGHT not be altruistic but the environment would benefit if we were all to plant a few trees in our lifetime. They may not need planting on our doorstep or in our own backyard, but they certainly are needed in parts of the world, such as the Amazon basin, where deforestation is a major problem and where, in places, non-sustainable farming threatens to leave arid unusable plains. Yet so much of our time is spent dealing with the immediate needs of family, work and day-to-day living that it does not leave us much time to think further than the end of our street.

Perhaps you could make a donation to an environmental charity, a tree-planting plan or a pollution clean-up scheme. Maybe you would enjoy an activity holiday where you join with others to rebuild a dry-stone wall or clean up a river. Whichever you decide, one thing is true – we would all feel a sense of satisfaction if occasionally we thought about and acted on some Grand Ideas or ideals. Like Piglet's haycorn, your actions might not make a difference in your lifetime, but they could to future generations.

VISUALISE YOURSELF SUCCEEDING LIKE POOH AND PIGLET, THEN WATCH IT HAPPEN

You tied a piece of string to Piglet, and you flew up to the letter-box, with the other end in your beak, and you pushed it through the wire and brought it down to the floor, and you and Pooh pulled hard at this end, and Piglet went slowly up the other end. And there you were.

THE HOUSE AT POOH CORNER

POOH AND PIGLET visualise a successful escape from Owl's storm-damaged home before actually making it happen. By contrast, Tigger consistently fails to think ahead or visualise the outcome of his actions, and gets into all sorts of scrapes. And Eeyore visualises failure, which becomes a self-fulfilling prophecy – it always does rain, he loses his house, and he is still sitting with his tail in the freezing stream long after Roo has been rescued. 'Well, it would happen,' remarks Eeyore. But how different it could be if Eeyore visualised success in the way that Pooh does.

Many sports stars have used visualisation to help them win – a technique that is applicable to all sports and to all aspects of life. So, how do you do it? It seems the best way is to separate the visualisation from the activity. You do not stand on the tennis court and visualise passing shots while playing, and neither do you sit at work and imagine yourself rising through the ranks until you alight in the chairman's office. There are self-help books on the subject and psychologists can assist you with visualisation techniques, but essentially you need to practise using your imagination.

Sit quietly and imagine yourself travelling home from work or shopping, going through your front door, and moving around in your home doing everyday tasks. You can practise imagining everyday objects too and really noticing what they look like. Recall events in which you did well and ones in which you did not do well, or where the outcome was not as you wished.

Next, practise visualising the area in which you want to improve or the activity at which you want to succeed, whether that's a better swimming technique or improving your posture or overall confidence. To do that, you need to picture yourself performing, for example, the perfect swimming stroke or passing tennis shot, or staying calm throughout pay negotiations and winning your rise – and so on. With the right practical preparation, mentally imaging how you will look and how you will do things can be transformed into actual performance. And that will be a Very Grand Thing!

Suddenly Christopher Robin began to laugh . . . and he laughed . . . and he laughed . . . and he laughed.

WINNIE-THE-POOH

CHILDREN LAUGH AND cry easily and are not inhibited by their need to do so, but as we grow up we become adept at suppressing this need. For most adults, episodes of rumbustious, uproarious laughter are rare. And that's a pity, because not only does laughter make you feel good, it also does you good.

There is truth in the maxim that 'Laughter is the best medicine'; it can help reduce stress, lower blood pressure and speed recovery. Laughter encourages the release of natural 'feel good' chemicals in the brain. This also seems to help reduce pain and increase the pain threshold so that lower doses of painkiller are needed, and is probably beneficial to the immune and endocrine (hormone) system. Happier people have been shown to suffer fewer colds than depressed, nervous or angry people. And studies on longevity show that laughter is an important ingredient for a long (and happy) life.

To benefit, seek out opportunities for laughter because in normal everyday life they do not occur very often. You would be surprised, and probably disappointed, if you counted the number of times you laughed during the day – for most adults it is not many. So make a regular date in your diary to meet friends with whom you know you will have a laugh. Or failing that, have a look through the TV and radio guide for programmes that genuinely get you giggling.

You could also try to laugh when things go wrong (not easy), to remind yourself to look for the funny side. It sometimes puts mishaps in perspective.

It's asking a lot, but you might try to smile at things that would ordinarily annoy you: thoughtless drivers, traffic jams, queues, other people interfering in what you are (best at) doing, unhelpful shop assistants, and so on.

The more it snows
(Tiddely pom),
The more it goes
(Tiddely pom),
The more it goes
(Tiddely pom),
On Snowing.

And nobody knows
(Tiddely pom),
How cold my toes
(Tiddely pom),
How cold my toes
(Tiddely pom),
Are growing.

THE HOUSE AT POOH CORNER

WITH OR WITHOUT Tiddely poms, poetry can bring enjoyment, and stimulate the imagination and emotions of people of all ages. So if you are not in the habit of 'humming' a poem as you go along, buy or borrow an anthology from the library or bookshop. Try one of those recommended for learning by heart or collections based on a theme that interests you.

Alternatively, buy yourself a note-book, pick up a pen and scribble down some poetry ideas of your own. However, '. . . *it isn't Easy*,' said Pooh to himself '. . . *because Poetry and hums aren't things which you get, they're things which get you.*' And all you can do is to go where they can find you.

In some studies, depressed people have found that expressing their feelings through poetry has relieved their mood and they have even been able to reduce medication. Maybe the therapeutic effects of writing verse will be helpful to you.

'Hallo, Eeyore,' said Christopher Robin, as he opened the door and came out. 'How are you?'
'It's snowing still,' said Eeyore gloomily.
'So it is.'
'And freezing.'
'Is it?'
'Yes,' said Eeyore. 'However,' he said brightening up a little, 'we haven't had an earthquake lately.'

THE HOUSE AT POOH CORNER

EEYORE'S PESSIMISM AND gloom are funny to read about. However, it is not so funny if you know someone just like Eeyore who spreads gloom, doom and despondency in your life, or if you feel like that yourself. (We are talking about a pessimistic outlook, not diagnosed depression that requires professional help.) But what can you do if you know someone like this, or if the way you interact with others casts a shadow over the sunniest day?

Some hypotheses blame gloom on an imbalance of nutrients, which a well-balanced healthy diet can correct. For many people, eating some chocolate instantaneously boosts their mood, but the effect is not as long-lasting as the mood-enhancing effect of exercise.

Physical activity results in the production of endorphins, the body's natural opiates that improve mood. Another mood-enhancing chemical called phenyl ethylamine (which only Owl might be able to spell, on a good day) is produced during exercise – it's a chemical found in chocolate and used to treat depression.

If you do want to feel less pessimistic you could also try adopting Pooh's positive mental attitude, or study and adopt a self-help technique that teaches you to think differently.

There was a small spinney of larch-trees just here, and it seemed as if the two Woozles, if that is what they were, had been going round this spinney; so round this spinney went Pooh and Piglet after them . . . Suddenly Winnie-the-Pooh stopped, and pointed excitedly in front of him. 'Look!' 'What?' said Piglet, with a jump . . . 'The tracks!' said Pooh. 'A third animal has joined the other two!'

WINNIE-THE-POOH

THINGS ARE NOT always as they seem. Pooh and Piglet were not on the track of Woozles or Wizzles, as they thought – they were tracking their own footprints in the snow, which left Pooh feeling rather foolish. It can be all too easy to jump to the wrong conclusion, particularly if you have a tendency towards jealousy or a suspicious nature. So be sure of the facts and check your evidence before you accuse anyone. Never go solely on snatches of overheard conversation or 'facts' reported by a third party. And try to put your preconceived ideas to one side when you are assessing what you have actually seen, heard, read or witnessed. Be as subjective and open as you can in your dealings with others – and yourself. If you don't you might be stalked by regrets, and they are harder to shake off than Woozles.

But Owl went on and on, using longer and longer words, until at last he came back to where he started . . .
For some time now Pooh had been saying 'Yes' and 'No' in turn, with his eyes shut, to all that Owl was saying, and having said, 'Yes, yes,' last time, he said, 'No, not at all,' now, without really knowing what Owl was talking about.

WINNIE-THE-POOH

POOH HAS LEARNT from experience that what Owl says is going to be in the main unintelligible and rather long and tedious, so he has also learnt that he need not listen because he is unlikely to miss anything of importance or relevance. The trouble is, once we stop listening we become vulnerable. If we don't listen to the safety announcement on the aeroplane because experience tells us it is always the same, then the time the airline decides to move the life jackets from under the seat to the chair pocket we will not know. If we do not listen to work colleagues and ensure we understand what they are saying, we can create discord and bad feeling and ultimately threaten our livelihood. When we stop listening to our partner,

a member of the family or a friend because we think we know what they are going to say, we put the relationship in jeopardy.

And it's not just listening that's important. Long-term relationships are dependent on good communication – it's a two-way process. Voicing our emotions, wants and needs and, equally importantly, listening to what we are being told or asked are essential for a healthy partnership. It is all too easy not to listen or to finish the sentences of others, either mentally or by speaking them out loud. Often we think we are being helpful when we do this. We use it as a way of acknowledging that we have experienced something similar. What we should really do is be quiet until the

other person has finished what they are trying to say. Only at that point is it appropriate to respond in a way that shows we have understood what has been said, or ask for clarification if we have not.

Asking further questions about what you have been told, and trying to find out how the other person feels, builds effective and purposeful conversation. Finding out what they want you to do is quite different from exchanging meaningless pleasantries. Keep those for the bus stop or supermarket queue, but communicate clearly with your family and friends.

Misunderstandings!

I could spend a happy morning
Seeing Roo,
I could spend a happy morning
Being Pooh.
For it doesn't seem to matter . . .

The sun was so delightfully warm, and the stone, which had been sitting in it for a long time, was so warm, too, that Pooh had almost decided to go on being Pooh in the middle of the stream for the rest for the morning . . .

The House at Pooh Corner

POOH IS THE ultimate daydreamer: sitting on a warm stone in the sun, daydreaming, is when he has his best ideas and composes his best Hums. Mind and brain experts call it 'incubation'. When your brain is relaxed you can focus fully on just one thing, as opposed to following several activities at once. And with all your brainpower at your disposal you are likely to have some inspirational thoughts. Daydreaming also allows the 'subconscious' to get to work, throwing up more ideas. Even if you do not find the answer to your current dilemma while you are daydreaming it might come to you later when your brain has been refreshed, because daydreams can be as restorative to the brain as a good sleep.

Don't feel guilty about siestas and power naps; you will function better for having them.

'Help, help!' cried Piglet, 'a Heffalump, a Horrible Heffalump!' and he scampered off as hard as he could, still crying out, 'Help, help, a Herrible Hoffalump! Hoff, Hoff, a Hellible Horralump! Holl, Holl, a Hoffable Hellerump!' And he didn't stop crying and scampering until he got to Christopher Robin's house.

WINNIE-THE-POOH

PANIC ATTACKS CAN happen at any time. You could be having fun at a party or shopping in a supermarket when your heart starts pounding, your mouth goes dry, you feel dizzy or unsteady and you experience very rapid breathing. These are just some of the symptoms. Trembling and shaking are common, together with pains in the chest, sweating, a feeling of choking and fear of losing control. No wonder some people rush to hospital, convinced they are having a heart attack – or in Piglet's case, to a place of safety such as Christopher Robin's house.

Of course you can feel panicky without ever experiencing a full-blown panic attack. In both cases the body experiences the fear response with a rush of adrenaline (the 'fight or flight' hormone). It can happen before a job interview, on a trip to the dentist or, in the case of a panic attack, for no obvious or appropriate reason. When this happens, slow down your breathing to avoid hyperventilation. This enables you to take control. Tell yourself it is 'only' a panic attack and it will pass and will not harm you. The attacks can be a one-off. However, if such attacks become disablingly frequent, you need longer-term strategies. Start by keeping a diary of emotional reactions and thoughts to try to recognise triggers. Seek help from your family doctor, who might suggest a course with a cognitive therapist and/or a clinical psychologist, or medication, to manage the symptoms.

However, most of the time our sense of panic either has no real cause or is a natural short-term event. The things we fear can be irrational. After all, Piglet could have avoided his panic and all the ho-ho hollering at his supposed Heffalump (that turned out to be Pooh with his head stuck in an empty honey jar), if he had learnt to appraise the situation calmly before hitting the panic button. He would also have saved himself later embarrassment – but then our irrational fears are often very hard to abandon.

'I see now,' said Winnie-the-Pooh.
'I have been Foolish and Deluded,' said he,
'and I am a Bear of No Brain at All.'
'You're the Best Bear in All the World,'
said Christopher Robin soothingly.
'Am I?' said Pooh hopefully. And then he
brightened up suddenly.

Winnie-the-Pooh

UNCONDITIONAL LOVE, SUCH as Christopher Robin gives Pooh, and nothing less is the only thing that will do when you make a complete mess of something. It's the kind of love that (ideally) parents give their children.

In the same way, true friends are the ones who are there when things go seriously wrong: when you have lost your job, are going through divorce, are suffering bereavement or are in financial difficulty. At times like these, you need someone who will listen to you in a non-judgemental way and offer practical help and advice, particularly if you are so emotionally involved that you are not thinking straight. You need encouragement,

hope and someone who will shore up your confidence. And similarly, you need to offer this to your friends when they are in need. If you have a friend who currently has a serious problem, put a note in your diary to check on them at regular intervals. Organise some informal outings or arrange when it is convenient to visit them, and take a picnic or a bottle of wine with you. Offer to do some shopping for them, take their dog for a walk or go with them while they walk their dog, as the exercise will do them good. Look after their home and cat so they can get away for a while. There are many ways to support friends in need.

31 | KNOWING THE DIFFERENCE BETWEEN BISCUIT COUGHS AND REAL COUGHS

'Nasty cold day,' said Rabbit, shaking his head. 'And you were coughing this morning.'
'How do you know?' said Roo indignantly.
'Oh, Roo, you never told me,' said Kanga reproachfully.
'It was a biscuit cough,' said Roo, 'not one you tell about.'

THE HOUSE AT POOH CORNER

AS READERS OF *The House at Pooh Corner* will know, Rabbit was telling a little fib, or gambling on Kanga's motherly tendency to worry enough to stop Roo going out on a cold, damp day. But the cameo above also highlights the fact that none of us wants to be ill (with the exception of those rare people who 'enjoy' bad health), and sometimes, if we are, we do not want to admit it or seek help.

While it is important not to waste the time of doctors by seeking treatment for self-limiting conditions such as colds and influenza, there are times when you should go to the doctor, for example, if the biscuit cough becomes persistent or is coupled with other symptoms that may indicate asthma or bronchitis or another serious condition that needs specialist treatment. Any unusual lumps or bumps, persistent conditions that have not responded to over-the-counter medicines recommended by a pharmacist, or inexplicable illnesses should be seen by your family doctor.

Don't take good health for granted. Look after both your own health and the health of those for whom you have some responsibilities, just as Kanga does. Do all you can to prevent illness through diet and exercise, particularly as you age. And if you are ill, inform yourself about your condition and try to follow doctors' orders.

*He [Pooh] had just come to the bridge;
and not looking where he was going, he
tripped over something, and the fir-cone
jerked out of his paw into the river.
'Bother,' said Pooh, as it floated slowly
under the bridge, and he went back to
get another fir-cone which had a rhyme
to it. But then he thought that he
would just look at the river instead,
because it was a peaceful sort of day, so
he lay down and looked at it, and it
slipped slowly away beneath him . . .
and suddenly, there was his fir-cone
slipping away too.
'That's funny,' said Pooh. 'I dropped it
on the other side,' said Pooh, 'and it
came out on this side! I wonder if it
would do it again?' And he went back
for some more fir-cones.
It did. It kept on doing it.*

THE HOUSE AT POOH CORNER

THE INVENTION OF Poohsticks, by Pooh, was accidental. You might well have played it yourself without knowing that Pooh invented the game and played it with Piglet and Christopher Robin. Standing on the wooden bridge at the edge of the Forest, each would drop a stick into the stream below, then cross the bridge to see whose stick emerged first on the other side.

But the accidental conception of Poohsticks in no way belittles its magnitude. In company with other great philosophers such as Archimedes, Pooh was observing a natural phenomenon. It was Archimedes, you will remember, who cried 'Eureka!' ('I've got it!') when he noticed that his bath overflowed as he got into it.* He then re-tested his observation to see if it was a repeatable phenomenon.

Likewise, Pooh found that the Poohsticks phenomenon was repeatable so he and the others went on to play it on many more occasions.

Make time yourself to look around you. Observe what's going on, notice the things that happen in your street, park, or where you work or study. Observation and finding time to stand and stare can teach us a lot. Continuing to be interested and wanting to carry on learning means you will use your faculties and be less likely to lose them.

*Archimedes is supposed to have leapt from his bath and run naked through the streets proclaiming 'Eureka!' Should you really need to know, Owl says the principle that Archimedes recognised was that the volume of a solid is equal to the volume of water it displaces when it is fully immersed.

*'When you wake up in the morning, Pooh,'
said Piglet at last, 'what's the first thing you
say to yourself?'*
*'What's for breakfast?' said Pooh. 'What do
you say, Piglet?'*
*'I say, I wonder what's going to happen
exciting to-day?' said Piglet.*
Pooh nodded thoughtfully.
'It's the same thing,' he said.

WINNIE-THE-POOH

POOH'S POSITIVE OPTIMISTIC outlook is beautifully characterised in his life-affirming start to each day. 'What's for breakfast?' you can hear him sighing with anticipation. Yes, breakfast is one of life's simple pleasures. For Pooh it is the start of another joyful day in which there will assuredly be honey for tea (as well as for breakfast, elevenses, luncheon, little smackerels, very nearly tea and, in all likelihood, supper and midnight feasts).

In common with Pooh, all breakfast-eaters enjoy a better mood, higher energy levels throughout the morning and better performance at school and work. Skipping breakfast increases the chances of weight problems, more serious obesity, developing diabetes or having a heart attack. People who eat breakfast every day are a third less likely to be obese compared with those who skip it. Those who eat wholegrain cereals every morning see the most benefits. Eating first thing in the morning stabilises blood sugar and regulates appetite and energy. So start each day the Pooh (Tigger and Piglet) way with enthusiasm and a healthy breakfast.

'Well, we must be getting home,' said Kanga.
'Good-bye, Pooh.' And in three large jumps
she was gone.
Pooh looked after her as she went.
'I wish I could jump like that,' he thought,
'Some can and some can't. That's how it is.'

WINNIE-THE-POOH

ONCE AGAIN, POOH has stated a universal truth based on his own observations. Some animals are more suited to certain activities than others. That applies to people, too. One key to happiness is surely being able to recognise and accept your limitations while fulfilling your potential within those limitations.

The secret of success in pursuing careers and hobbies is identifying the right niche for you and then trying your hardest to make it work. You're more likely to succeed and to therefore feel good about yourself for making the effort and you will enjoy greater self-confidence.

The Australians have turned Pooh's commonsense observation into a science by identifying which people (body types) are best suited to which sports (categorised by muscle type, physique, and so on). Their sporting academies of excellence are based on identifying potential sports stars at a young age so that they have a better chance of reaching international standards.

Pooh's intuition tells him that his physique is definitely not meant for jumping like Kanga (even though he enjoys passing the time practising jumps at the sandy place at the top of the Forest). Pooh is one of life's walkers. If, like Pooh, you are unlikely to be an international athlete, you will still want to find a physical activity that you like because you need to take regular exercise for health and weight control. Your chosen activities also have to fit in with your lifestyle if you are to succeed at getting fitter and not getting fatter.

'Did you see me swimming?' squeaked Roo excitedly, while Kanga scolded him and rubbed him down. 'Pooh, did you see me swimming? That's called swimming, what I was doing. Rabbit, did you see what I was doing? Swimming. Hallo, Piglet! I say, Piglet! What do you think I was doing! Swimming! . . .'

WINNIE-THE-POOH

THERE IS SCOPE in most people's lives to become more physically active. Obviously this book is not a physical fitness manual – you can find more detailed advice elsewhere. But Pooh can certainly point to the wisdom of taking exercise. There are three types of exercise – AEROBIC, STRENGTH TRAINING and FLEXIBILITY – and they all benefit your everyday life, health and vitality.

Any exercise should start with a gentle warm-up of around ten minutes to raise the core temperature of the working muscles, and end with a so-called warm-down and stretch of around five minutes to help prevent post-exercise soreness.

If you have not done any or much activity for some time, it is important to build up slowly over a period of weeks. If in doubt, or if you have existing medical conditions, talk to your GP or ask a practice nurse for advice before starting.

Aerobic or cardiovascular exercise such as swimming strengthens the heart and improves the body's ability to extract oxygen from the blood and transport it around the body. This also helps you burn fat for weight control and has other health benefits. Other examples are brisk walking, like Pooh; jogging along, like Tigger; swimming (not quite like Roo); rowing (similar to Christopher Robin and Pooh in an umbrella); working on gym equipment and other activities carried out to a moderately intensive level of exertion. Start gradually, if necessary with just five minutes of activity, building it up to a minimum of thirty-minute sessions on most days of the week (or one hour daily, if you can manage it). You will find that regular exercise increases self-confidence and gives you more energy.

You can also use walking, cycling and jogging to exercise while exploring the area in which you live and to visit friends, as Pooh does. Obtain a map from the local council of cycle or walking routes and, when you have time, build in visits to places of interest. If you plan bigger expeditions and longer walks off the beaten track, perhaps while on holiday, invest in Ordnance Survey maps, all-weather clothing, the right footwear, a compass and even survival equipment. And don't forget to pack water and provisions in case of emergency.

IN WHICH WE FLEX THE NECESSARY DORSAL MUSCLES: STRENGTH TRAINING

Owl, who was admiring his letter-box, flew down again. Together they pushed and pulled at the armchair, and in a little while Pooh came out from underneath, and was able to look round him again.

THE HOUSE AT POOH CORNER

LIFTING LARGE STONE honey pots is hard work that requires strength. And strength is achieved by resistance training to make muscles stronger. The resistance comes from working with free (hand-held) weights (heavy cans or honey jars will do), or in the gym working on weight machines. Equally, you can increase strength by resisting against your own body weight, as in press-ups, lunges and squats. Building more muscle also means that you have the potential to burn more calories. And that is a Fine Thing.

He had made up a little hum that very morning, as he was doing his Stoutness Exercises in front of the glass: Tra-la-la, *as he stretched up as high as he could go, and then* Tra-la-la, tra-la – oh, help! – la, *as he tried to reach his toes.*

WINNIE-THE-POOH

STRETCHING EXERCISES LENGTHEN muscles (as opposed to weight or resistance training which builds bulk). Flexibility is important for simple everyday tasks such as reaching honey from the top shelf of your cupboard and for sport such as tennis, or yoga relaxation exercises. Muscles need to be warmed up before they can be stretched, so do not try to stretch before you have warmed up for five to ten minutes.

Yoga and Pilates improve flexibility, as well as muscle strength and tone – particularly 'core' strength and stability. The muscles that build core strength are abdominal, lower back and pelvic muscles. By strengthening these, you have a stronger 'core' which stabilises the whole body and provides support and structure to the spine and for all movements.

In addition to better balance and body control, if you work on stretching and flexibility through yoga and the original system of Pilates you can also increase your sense of well-being.

Piglet had got up early that morning to pick himself a bunch of violets; and when he had picked them and put them in a pot in the middle of his house, it suddenly came over him that nobody had ever picked Eeyore a bunch of violets, and the more he thought of this, the more he thought how sad it was to be an Animal who had never had a bunch of violets picked for him.

THE HOUSE AT POOH CORNER

SO PIGLET RUSHED off, feeling happy, to Eeyore's gloomy place. But, as is the way of the world, it didn't turn out quite as Piglet hoped. First he was scolded by Eeyore, then he was the butt of Eeyore's bitterness, and finally Piglet was scorned and became the subject of Eeyore's unkind sarcasm.

Even though it is natural to want to retaliate, Piglet did not. Like a Knight of Old he abandoned neither his courtesy nor his quest. He held true to his errand, behaved graciously, and laid his bunch of violets at Eeyore's feet (or should we say hooves) before scampering off.

Piglet's behaviour is an example to us all. He did not lose his temper and so he had nothing to regret. He knew he had shown Eeyore an act of kindness and he could feel happy about that.

And later, when Eeyore had got over his disappointment, he would notice Piglet's violets, remember his kindness and feel less gloomy.

'Let's go and see everybody,' said Pooh . . .
Piglet thought that they ought to have a
Reason for going to see everybody, like
Looking for Small or Organizing an
Expotition, if Pooh could think of
something.
Pooh could.
'We'll go because it's Thursday,' he said,
'and we'll go to wish everybody a Very
Happy Thursday. Come on, Piglet.'

THE HOUSE AT POOH CORNER

SPONTANEITY MIGHT NOT be highly regarded in books dealing with social etiquette. Etiquette demands a more formal system of invitation and acceptance at appointed times. So somehow, when people say, 'You must come and see us when you are passing,' or 'Do drop in,' it is difficult to know if they really mean it. Some do, some don't. But there's no harm in taking them at their word. After all, at worst they will not be at home or they might hide behind the sofa pretending not to be in and at best, they will be pleased to see you. Even the mood of gloomy old Eeyore could be mildly elevated by surprise visitors.

If the idea of a more spontaneous social life appeals to you then do try it. But make sure that in return for you 'taking people as you find them', you are also willing to be 'dropped in on'. When you go visiting unannounced, make sure you go prepared. Take a comestible or two for spontaneous smakerels and try to have lots of interesting things to talk about or news to share. Acting spontaneously and enjoying others' spontaneity has a liberating effect on your life and opens up a world of new possibilities – a very good route if ever there was one to a greater sense of well-being.

Finally, don't be upset if you misjudge the recipient of your spontaneity, who might not want to see you at that moment. You might just have caught them on a bad day!

Balancing on three legs, he [Eeyore] *began to bring his fourth leg very cautiously up to his ear. 'I did this yesterday,' he explained, as he fell down for the third time. 'It's quite easy . . .'*

WINNIE-THE-POOH

WHETHER YOU ARE a pachyderm like Eeyore, or any other type of thick-skinned animal, you could undoubtedly benefit from practising yoga positions such as the Down Dog, the Tortoise or the Standing Tree to improve suppleness in your joints, strengthen your core muscles and focus your mind on not falling over. Yoga offers a unique combination of mind and body benefits. You can choose the style of yoga that suits your needs. Some put more emphasis on the asanas (yoga postures) and others spend more time on pranayama (breathing) or meditation. As a rough guide, the two types that are most likely to provide a vigorous physical workout are Astanga and Bikram. For a gentler focus on posture and precision try Iyengar. To concentrate on meditation, spirituality and the mind–body connection sample Kundalini, and if you fancy the yoga lifestyle, with postures, breathing, meditation and a modicum of chanting, go for Sivananda yoga. A combination of several types of yoga in a more westernised style is generally described as Hatha yoga, the type you are most likely to find at a local evening class.

The benefits claimed for yoga are increased flexibility and strength, toned muscles, deeper relaxation and better posture. And all that for around twenty minutes a day.

Here's a yoga pose to reduce stress. It involves lying flat on your back on the floor with your arms out to the sides at shoulder level and your knees raised and feet together flat on the floor. Breathe in, then breathe out, pulling your stomach strongly towards your spine. Lift your knees to your chest then lower towards the floor on the right at a right angle to your torso. Hold the position while breathing rhythmically (two to three breaths, working up to twelve) and relaxing your upper body completely. Bring your knees up to your chest once more, then lower and repeat on the left. There, Eeyore, you should find that one easier . . .

> *By-and-by Pooh and Piglet came along. Pooh was telling Piglet in a singing voice that it didn't seem to matter, if he didn't get any fatter, and he didn't* think *he was getting any fatter . . .*

THE HOUSE AT POOH CORNER

BEING OVERWEIGHT AND being underweight are both bad for health. But what about being stout like Pooh? There is a difference. Stocky or muscular people may appear to be overweight with the fashion for being slim, but if you are fit then it is healthier to be stout and fit than slim and unfit.

One way of finding out if you are a healthy weight is to calculate your body mass index (BMI), which is more sophisticated than just knowing your weight. To work out your BMI measure your height in metres and multiply the figure by itself.

Then measure your weight in kilograms. Divide the weight by the height squared (i.e. the first number you worked out).

Then see how you measure up below . . .

BODY MASS INDEX

Less than 18.5	Underweight
18.5–24	Normal range
25+	Overweight
30–34	Obese
35–39	Very obese
40+	Extremely obese

If your BMI is at the top end of the optimum range, or perhaps outside it, but you are physically fit, then you probably have no excess risk of chronic diseases such as high blood pressure, heart disease and stroke.

An even more accurate way of finding out if you have too much body fat, as opposed to being stocky, is to use body-fat monitor scales. Health clubs, gyms and slimming clubs have these and it may be that your doctor's surgery could invest in some – do they have a suggestions box? In addition to displaying weight they can also tell us what percentage of our body weight is fat, muscle and water, and that's what really counts.

So even though Pooh may appear stout, so long as he has a reasonable body-fat ratio and he is fit he has nothing to be concerned about.

What shall we do about poor little Tigger?
If he never eats nothing he'll never get bigger.
He doesn't like honey and haycorns and thistles
Because of the taste and because of the bristles.
And all the good things which an animal likes
Have the wrong sort of swallow or too
many spikes.

THE HOUSE AT POOH CORNER

WHICH IS A PITY, because if Tigger did only one thing to improve his diet (and therefore health) it would be to eat at least five portions* of fruit and vegetables each day. And the same applies to you. Eating more fruit and vegetables is the one improvement that most people could benefit from. It is also one of the easiest ways to achieve better health. It has been estimated that five portions of fruit and vegetables a day could prevent up to twenty per cent of deaths from heart disease and certain cancers. So, if you are a bit more adventurous in the greengrocer's department you will discover that not all vegetables and fruits have the wrong sort of swallow or too many spikes and, indeed, many can add colour, taste and texture to your food.

Fruit in particular is a convenient snack food, and included in the five-a-day could be portions of frozen and canned fruits and vegetables, plus fruit and vegetable juices. Some specialist medical researchers consider five a day to be the bare minimum and encourage a higher consumption of around nine a day. But most of us have to get to five first.

In general a portion equals eighty grams or just over three ounces, or the equivalent of one handful, or three tablespoons in the case of cooked or canned vegetables and fruit.

'I think *that I have just remembered something. I have just remembered something that I forgot to do yesterday and shan't be able to do to-morrow. So I suppose I really ought to go back and do it now.'*
'*We'll do it this afternoon, and I'll come with you,' said Pooh.*
'*It isn't the sort of thing you can do in the afternoon,' said Piglet quickly. 'It's a very particular morning thing, that has to be done in the morning, and, if possible, between the hours of – What would you say the time was?'*
'*About twelve,' said Winnie-the-Pooh, looking at the sun.*
'*Between, as I was saying, the hours of twelve and twelve five. So, really, dear old Pooh, if you'll excuse me . . . '*

WINNIE-THE-POOH

PIGLET FEARS THAT a Woozle is about to pounce on him (and Pooh), so he prepares to flee. In fact Piglet lives in a permanent, but intermittent, state of fear about attacks from Hostile or Fierce Animals and being bounced on by Tigger. This state of mind is shared by many people today who feel rather small and powerless in the face of fears as diverse as going to work, financial insecurity, taking on the risk of a new intimate relationship or getting on a plane.

While we would be right to follow Piglet's example and run away from hostile animals, there are some fears we would benefit from learning to deal with.

Being prepared by thinking through what you might do in situations that cause you to be fearful can be helpful. It might seem extreme, but thinking through the actions you would need to take if you were in a car accident, or stuck in a lift, or locked in a building overnight (or whatever your particular 'worst case scenario' might be), could really help. Finding out more about anything you fear can help you reduce and manage that fear.

Learn from your own experiences, too. Relive how you have coped in situations that might have been fearful to others. Read about the ordeals of people involved in disasters. It might seem ghoulish, but the newspapers and magazines are full of people's personal tales of survival and their triumph over tragedies of all sorts, from illnesses such as cancer to surviving shipwrecks. You might find that many of these people have something in common – they refuse to be victims. Instead, they become proactive and in some cases use their experience to help others in similar situations.

Other practical steps could be to see a psychologist or a medically qualified hypnotist to overcome your fears. Or if, for example, you have a fear of flying, use a holiday to take a course to confront and help overcome that fear.

Piglet overcame his fears when he allowed himself to be hauled up to Owl's letterbox. Pooh overcame his fears when he rescued Piglet from the flood. Tigger overcame his fears when he 'fell' out of the tree into Christopher Robin's tunic (and learned to trust others to keep him safe). Take heart, you can do it too.

He [Small, a Very Small Beetle] *had been staying with Christopher Robin for a few seconds, and he had started round a gorse-bush for exercise, but instead of coming back the other way, as expected, he hadn't, so nobody knew where he was.*
'I expect he's just gone home,' said Christopher Robin to Rabbit.
'Did he say Good-bye-and-thank-you-for-a-nice-time?' said Rabbit.
'He's only just said how-do-you-do,' said Christopher Robin.
'Ha!' said Rabbit. After thinking a little, he went on: 'Has he written a letter saying how much he enjoyed himself, and how sorry he was he had to go so suddenly?'
Christopher Robin didn't think he had.
'Ha!' said Rabbit again, and looked very important. 'This is Serious. He is Lost. We must begin the Search at once.'

THE HOUSE AT POOH CORNER

OF COURSE, SMALL was not lost. And the moral of that, in descending order of importance, is . . .

- Don't jump to conclusions (Rabbit).

- Always remember to leave detailed instructions of where you can be contacted (Small).

- Remember to say thank you for having me (whoever you are and however important you are).

Telling people when you are leaving an event, or where you can be contacted when you go on holiday is not only good manners, it is important for other reasons. If your home is burgled or a relative is taken ill, then you can be contacted more easily. And if, for example, you are going on a trek to watch Grizzly Bears in the Rockies or are crossing the Arctic on foot to (re)discover the North Pole, and you do not emerge from the forest or at the Arctic shelter at the specified or estimated time, then there will be a greater chance of rescue in cases of emergency.

No matter how well you know these things they are easily and periodically forgotten, so do try to bear them in mind.

. . . Christopher Robin called 'Halt!' and they all sat down and rested.
'I think,' said Christopher Robin, 'that we ought to eat all our Provisions now, so that we shan't have so much to carry.'
'Eat all our what?' said Pooh.
'All that we've brought,' said Piglet, getting to work.
'That's a good idea,' said Pooh and he got to work too.

WINNIE-THE-POOH

THERE ARE MANY situations in which we need to take a break from what we are doing to refresh ourselves, rest or eat. Without proper breaks we simply make more mistakes. In some situations we even endanger ourselves and others, hence the stark reminders on motorways that Tiredness Kills and the injunctions to Take a Break.

The British culture of working through lunch is of no benefit to anyone. You need to take a breather and eat a nutritious light lunch so that you feel and perform your best as the day wears on. You can take a break from office or other work in other ways. Deep breathing is a simple and effective technique for refreshing yourself and reducing stress. Breathing in deeply and evenly to a count of five or ten (whichever suits you), then releasing to the same count for up to ten times is a useful way to restore your equilibrium and calm.

Caffeine in coffee and cola drinks may be valuable to help keep drivers alert on long journeys. However, too much (and sensitivity varies between individuals) can be over-stimulating to your adrenal system and will keep your blood pressure raised. If, for example, you drink coffee or cola all day at work you could end up edgy and nervy and less able to cope. So replace some with water or (diluted) fruit juice. Taking a walk or a twenty-minute bike ride at lunchtime – or even a short massage – will help clear the mind and raise energy levels for the afternoon. And if your workplace is noisy, try to escape to a quieter place during your breaks. If you take regular and effective breaks you will be less likely to experience headaches, fatigue, anxiety and other negative effects associated with ignoring the need for R&R (rest and recuperation).

'Have you seen Piglet?'
'Yes,' said Pooh. 'I suppose that isn't any good either?' he asked meekly.
'Well, it depends if he saw anything.'
'He saw me,' said Pooh.
Rabbit sat down on the ground next to Pooh, and, feeling much less important like that, stood up again.

THE HOUSE AT POOH CORNER

YOU CAN USE body language to your advantage, just as Rabbit does, although not necessarily always to dominate. When meeting people, make sure you send out the right signals; you may feel friendly and approachable on the inside, but your body language may contradict that. Since others can only interpret your intentions by what they see and hear you do, it is best to try to send out the right signals so that you do not appear aloof, unfriendly or insignificant.

Move forward to greet people and lean forward when starting to talk so that you look interested. Make eye contact and be responsive, encouraging the speaker with nods and facial expressions. Have an open stance – crossed arms and legs give the impression of being defensive, scared or unlikely to listen. And smile!

Mind games are as important as physical postures when it comes to influencing others. Repetition of phrases such as 'I can and I will' before meetings and events helps some people. Positive thoughts such as 'I can handle this' all help enhance your self-belief and confidence. If you do not believe that you have a valuable contribution to make or that you will come out on top when necessary, then you are sabotaging your own game plan or career.

    But the more Tigger put his nose into this and his paw into that, the more things he found which Tiggers didn't like. And when he had found everything in the cupboard, and couldn't eat any of it, he said to Kanga, 'What happens now?'
But Kanga and Christopher Robin and Piglet were all standing round Roo, watching him have his Extract of Malt. And Roo was saying, 'Must I?' and Kanga was saying, 'Now, Roo dear, you remember what you promised.'
'What is it?' whispered Tigger to Piglet.
'His Strengthening Medicine,' said Piglet. 'He hates it.'

THE HOUSE AT POOH CORNER

BUT IT TURNED out to be What Tiggers Like. So Tigger went to live at Kanga's house where he had Extract of Malt for breakfast, dinner and tea, and when Kanga thought he wanted strengthening, he had a spoonful or two of Roo's breakfast after meals as medicine. Which is all very well, except that if Tigger stopped being a faddy eater and instead ate a varied diet he – like you – would not need dietary supplements.

Vitamin pills might seem like a short cut to health, but it doesn't work like that. The vitamins, minerals, fibre and other beneficial substances in fruit, vegetables, wholegrains and other nutritious foods all work together to reduce the risk of chronic diseases. Dietary supplements alone cannot do that and, in some cases, taking nutrients in isolation can be harmful.

However, if you don't eat a well-balanced diet, there is an argument to say that multi-vitamin and mineral supplements can help you stay as full of bounce as Tigger. Two leading researchers at Harvard Medical School's department of public health reviewed research on multi-vitamins in 2002. They concluded in the *Journal of the American Medical Association* that 'inadequate intake of several vitamins has been linked to chronic diseases, including coronary heart disease, cancer and osteoporosis . . . we recommend that all adults take one multivitamin daily.' If you follow their advice, choose a product offering around 100 per cent RDA (that's the recommended daily amount), and steer clear of mega-doses.

Note: Incidentally, Extract of Malt is still added to some baby and invalid foods. So what does it have to recommend it? It keeps indefinitely (useful when you live in a forest far from shops) and it is a rich source of the minerals iron and zinc, and a moderate source of Vitamin B3 (niacin), all vital for energy – and Tigger has plenty of that.

Suddenly Christopher Robin began to tell Pooh about some of the things: People called Kings and Queens and something called Factors, and a place called Europe, and an island in the middle of the sea where no ships came, and how you make a Suction Pump (if you want to), and when Knights were Knighted, and what comes from Brazil. And Pooh, his back against one of the sixty-something trees, and his paws folded in front of him, said 'Oh!' and 'I don't know,' and thought how wonderful it would be to have a Real Brain which could tell you things.

THE HOUSE AT POOH CORNER

THE OLD ADAGE 'If you don't use it you will lose it' applies as much to your brainpower as to muscle power – all parts of your body need exercising.

There is great reward in a lifetime of learning. Anything that you enjoy and that makes you think and gets you excited means you are really using your brain cells. Even though Pooh protests that he is a bear of little brain, he doesn't do too badly when it comes to composing Hums. They excite him and he practises composing poetry quite frequently, so he is good at it. If you can find something that is a concentrated effort and interactive and fun to do then your brainpower will increase and you will find that your memory improves too.

Leisure activities such as board games, crosswords and puzzles all help you stay mentally sharp, but the ultimate mental challenge for most of us is probably learning a new language.

The best time for a brain workout can be morning or evening, depending on whether you are a proverbial lark (Pooh) or owl (Wol). But when you are tired or after a big meal you will find your brain is not at its best.

We can even learn by watching others, sometimes called vicarious learning. Traditional examples are master classes in subjects such as music and acting, and trainee doctors sitting in during a qualified doctor's consultation with a patient. We can also use radio and TV shows for vicarious learning by watching gardening, do-it-yourself or cookery programmes if we put what we have learned into practice.

'But there are twelve pots of honey in my cupboard, and they've been calling to me for hours. I couldn't hear them properly before because Rabbit would talk, but if nobody says anything except those twelve pots, I think, Piglet, I shall know where they're coming from. Come on.'

THE HOUSE AT POOH CORNER

WHEN RABBIT AND Pooh and Piglet are lost in the mist, due to Rabbit's over-confidence and poor sense of direction, Pooh is the one who knows the way. However, Rabbit keeps chattering so that Pooh cannot think or have the quiet he needs to tune into his inner voice. And because Pooh is humble and does not demand 'Quiet!', his valuable store of intuitive wisdom remains unused.

Rabbit and Owl, who love to hear the sound of their own voices, are frequently guilty of ignoring the wisdom of others. If you suspect you are one of those people who talk incessantly, try to curb your chat long enough for others to voice their thoughts and opinions. Learn to accept silence in conversations – it is natural and permissible.

And the next time you are lost in the fog (spiritually or logistically), try to be quiet and listen to your innate sense of direction. Let it be your indicator for left or right as it is for right and wrong.

'I think not to-day, dear. Another day.'
'To-morrow?' said Roo hopefully.
'We'll see,' said Kanga.
'You're always seeing, and nothing
ever happens,' said Roo sadly.

THE HOUSE AT POOH CORNER

BE CAREFUL WHEN you make promises, especially to children and anyone you care about. Children have to take things literally. They know only what you tell them and they are intellectually defenceless.

A child is not (as many people think) a small adult. Added to which, children have long and accurate memories and a strong sense of right and wrong. Children need and deserve rewards and recognition for their efforts. So don't let them down (not that Kanga ever let Roo down). Let them have jam when you have promised it. Immediate rewards are likely to reinforce good behaviour in children, and good performance in adults (but, of course, they should not always be sweets). Similarly, remember promises made to adult family members and friends. Reward them too for efforts they have made on your behalf.

And don't forget yourself. Give yourself little rewards when you deserve them. Pooh often rewards himself with 'little somethings' and so should you. For example, if you have taken up – and better still stuck with – an exercise regime or made a sustained effort to eat more healthily, or worked hard, treat yourself to an item of clothing or a CD or a book you have been meaning to read – and give yourself the time to read it.

Sing Ho! for the life of a Bear!
Sing Ho! for the life of a Bear!
I don't much mind if it rains or snows,
'Cos I've got a lot of honey on my nice new nose!
I don't much care if it snows or thaws,
'Cos I've got a lot of honey on my nice clean paws!
Sing Ho! for a Bear!
Sing Ho! for a Pooh!
And I'll have a little something in an hour or two!

WINNIE-THE-POOH

POOH'S SONGS ARE a source of great pleasure to him (and us). Like most artistes Pooh finds composition difficult, but the reward of a shiny new song to sing as he stomps through the Forest makes the effort worthwhile.

Do you have enough music in your life? Music can both soothe and excite. It can release the tension of everyday life so much that it can even help lower blood pressure and change the pattern of brainwaves to make your thinking more creative. (The right kind of music, for example, Mozart, could enhance Christopher Robin's performance if played while he is working out factors and logarithms.) How all this works is something of a mystery, but it is likely that the different rhythms and other characteristics of music stimulate different parts of the brain in the same way that natural body chemicals affect our emotions and our basic appetites.

Use music to help you relax or play it to stimulate creativity when you have to do some creative writing, perhaps a speech or a letter or an application for a job. Play some lively music if you want to keep your concentration while driving. Put on some calming Gregorian chants when you need to check your bank and credit card statements . . . then have a stiff drink and a lie-down.

Of course, music can be as irritating as it can be soothing, particularly if it is another person's choice of music played too loudly at a time when you want peace and quiet – in which case it sends the blood pressure and heart rate soaring. Don't get mad, get earplugs – or suggest the listener uses headphones.

Alternatively, have a go at singing yourself. Choral singing is a joyous and beneficial social activity – and not all choirs audition or require you to read music. Singing improves breathing and helps tone those face and tummy muscles, and to sing well you have to improve your posture and release tension in your neck and shoulders! It improves your listening skills because you have to really listen to a tune before singing it. Singing helps release emotions and it will improve the clarity of your speech, as you need to be careful with diction for words to be understood when you sing. It is no coincidence that we sing when we are happy – singing makes you feel good.

You can imagine Piglet's joy when at last the ship came in sight of him. In after-years he liked to think that he had been in Very Great Danger during the Terrible Flood, but the only danger he had really been in was the last half-hour of his imprisonment, when Owl, who had just flown up, sat on a branch of his tree to comfort him, and told him a very long story about an aunt who had once laid a seagull's egg by mistake, and the story went on and on, rather like this sentence, until Piglet who was listening out of his window without much hope, went to sleep quietly and naturally, slipping slowly out of the window towards the water until he was only hanging on by his toes, at which moment, luckily, a sudden loud squawk from Owl, which was really part of the story, being what his aunt said, woke the Piglet up and just gave him time to jerk himself back into safety . . .

WINNIE-THE-POOH

POOR PIGLET, NOT only is he marooned in a flood but then he is bored to stupefaction by one of Owl's long and tedious anecdotes while waiting for rescue. There are several other instances when Piglet and Pooh nearly give up the will to live during one of Owl's narratives. But in dozing off they are doing the right thing. What better use of the time than to have a power nap? Daytime naps can be as refreshing as a night's sleep.

Next time your energy is flagging, or you are trying to ignore a very boring person and you feel your head flopping forward – give in to it (as long as it's not your boss). A siesta of fifteen minutes keeps you going for longer. It increases alertness, productivity, creativity and problem-solving later in the day. Added to that, a daytime sleep when you need it does more for you than an extra hour or more of sleep at night. But don't nap for longer than twenty minutes because after that you go into deep sleep and being woken from that will leave you groggy, muddled and less alert.

The Piglet was sitting on the ground at the door of his house blowing happily at a dandelion, and wondering whether it would be this year, next year, sometime or never.

WINNIE-THE-POOH

WHEN WE TRY to sit down on the floor, or on the ground, our joints are rather stiff and we quickly experience pins and needles and we feel uncomfortable.

But, the more you practise getting into lots of odd positions the more flexible your joints will be and they will stay that way for longer. Start making a habit of sitting on the floor, or on a rug on the ground for a picnic rather than using chairs. Interestingly, you might find it gives you a different, more relaxed perspective on what is going on around you.

There are other simple exercises you can do, too, to improve or maintain joint flexibility. See how quickly you can rise up and down ten times from a chair (or the loo) just using your leg muscles, not pushing off with your arms. Do this daily to strengthen muscles and increase endurance. Do simple exercises to strengthen wrist, hip and spine such as lifting light weights or doing a few press-ups. Every time the muscles pull on bones they stimulate blood to that area for bone production. Try stretching exercises, aquarobics, yoga or Pilates under the guidance of a well-qualified instructor. And work at maintaining or improving your balance. Start by trying to walk along a straight line, heel to toe. Not as easy as it seems, is it? But you know what they say about practice . . .

'. . . – the news has worked through to my corner of the Forest – the damp bit down on the right which nobody wants . . .'

THE HOUSE AT POOH CORNER

EEYORE IS SOLEMN and gloomy and has never been known to express irrational exuberance. He lives in a Gloomy Place, which he describes as a cold, wet and ugly corner. His presence usually puts a damper on proceedings. To those who know him, just a glimpse is enough to provoke, with a sigh, 'Poor old Eeyore.' And newcomers to the Forest are told 'You musn't mind Eeyore, he is always gloomy.' However, if Eeyore were to move to the Mediterranean (or a lighter and brighter part of the Forest) he might brighten up in himself: Pooh's mood lifts as he leaves Eeyore's gloomy corner to go in search of Eeyore's tail and catches the sight of blue sky between soft clouds.

We all need light in our lives. Daylight must fall on the back of the eye where receptors use it to stimulate the production of hormones that regulate our body clocks to fit with the natural rhythms of the day. Dimming light in the evening allows melatonin hormone levels to rise to make us feel drowsy. We need sunlight on our skin for the body to produce Vitamin D for strong teeth and bones. And lack of daylight during short days and long dark winter nights can make us feel gloomy and, in extreme cases, causes Seasonal Affective Disorder (SAD).

Lighten your life. Ensure your rooms are well lit (and airy too), try natural daylight light bulbs, and if you have trouble waking in the morning try a dawn-simulator alarm clock that gradually brightens the room to daylight to wake you.

Try to get out into the Forest yourself for a twenty- to thirty-minute walk every day, if you can. Remember to wear a sunscreen of at least SPF 15 and avoid the peak UV hours during the hottest part of the day.

THINK YOURSELF FIT (OR THINNER, OR WHATEVER ELSE YOU WOULD LIKE TO BE)

Now, by this time Rabbit wanted to go for a walk too, and finding the front door full, he went out by the back door, and came round to Pooh, and looked at him. 'Hallo, are you stuck?' he asked. 'N-no,' said Pooh carelessly. 'Just resting and thinking and humming to myself.'

WINNIE-THE-POOH

SOMETIMES POOH IS more given to thinking than doing, so it is a great pity that he did not know about the following mind-over-body technique when he found himself in a tight spot in Rabbit's front door. It is a technique that in experiments has been shown to give muscles a workout without moving a muscle. It seems that just imagining yourself exercising can increase the strength of large muscles such as the thighs and biceps and even the *gluteus maximus* (bottom). Volunteers in one experiment had to imagine flexing specific muscles as hard as possible while lying down.

They did these 'training' sessions five times a week. Other volunteers did nothing. By measuring electrical brain activity and nerve impulses at the arm muscles, for example, the researchers could check that the subjects were not cheating by actually flexing their muscles. After five weeks of 'training', muscle strength was increased in those who did the mental workouts and the strength improvement lasted three months. A very appealing method of strength training for a bear given to doing nothing in the most constructive way possible.

Pooh was sitting in his house one day, counting his pots of honey, when there came a knock on the door.

'Fourteen,' said Pooh. 'Come in. Fourteen. Or was it fifteen? Bother. That's muddled me.'

'Hallo, Pooh,' said Rabbit.

'Hallo, Rabbit. Fourteen, wasn't it?'

'What was?'

'My pots of honey what I was counting.'

'Fourteen, that's right.'

'Are you sure?'

'No,' said Rabbit. 'Does it matter?'

'I just like to know,' said Pooh humbly. 'So as I can say to myself: "I've got fourteen pots of honey left." Or fifteen, as the case may be. It's sort of comforting.'

THE HOUSE AT POOH CORNER

EVERYONE HAS A need for financial security – and at the least it is, as Pooh says, nice to know where you stand. But in order to feel a degree of financial and, therefore, personal security you need a medium- to long-term plan. This might sound very tedious and boring, or even incomprehensible for a Bear of Very Little Brain, but once it is achieved you will relax and might even feel rather smug for having done it.

Being aware of your financial position might help prevent unplanned spending sprees. You know the sort of thing – you have a bad day at work, a lot of stress in your personal life, so you go out and spend money that you had not planned to spend. It makes you feel better for a short while but then the feeling turns to guilt, and it may even have repercussions that lead to further work or domestic problems. It's estimated that £5.4 billion is spent annually in the UK on such unplanned 'stress spending'. Maybe you should leave your credit card at home on days when you feel that might happen, or treat yourself to a cheaper little something instead.

And by the way, is your credit card giving you the deal that's right for you, or is it time to change? It may be worth arranging to meet an independent financial advisor to talk about savings and so on. Choose an advisor who is accredited and not one who is paid by commission or by your bank or mortgage provider. Before you meet, try to assess what sort of 'financial personality' you have – are you prepared to take risks in an investment or would that worry you? Think about whether ethical investments are important to you. Get the advisor to match the plan to your personal tolerance of risk as well as your long-term financial needs. What's best for you – bonds, stock market, property, gold?

Sounds rather grand, but we each need to spread our investment bets and build the best portfolio we can. Even if you are only in your twenties, you are on the road to retirement and you need to map your way as carefully as possible – that way you can afford more fun along the way and fewer nasty surprises around hidden bends and dips en route. Bon voyage.

'Good morning, Eeyore,' said Pooh. 'Good morning, Pooh Bear,' said Eeyore gloomily. 'If it is *a good morning,' he said. 'Which I doubt,' said he.*

WINNIE-THE-POOH

EXPECT THE WORST and you will never be disappointed, in fact you should usually be pleasantly surprised that things do not turn out as bad as you feared. Some people find this logic works for them. Eeyore, for one, would probably be happier if he decided not to live his life as if the sword of Damocles were suspended above his head by a single horsehair. If he came out from beneath his self-inflicted cloud of doom and tried to stop expecting anything from a heavy downpour to an earthquake or apocalypse, he would feel a lot better, and he would probably suffer fewer sniffles, coughs and colds. That is because your mind can influence many of your body systems, including your immune system.

This scientifically proven relationship has been given a long, impressive name (that probably only Owl can spell) to show its importance: psychoneuroimmunology. Medical experts with equally long impressive names such as neuroendocrinologists (brain-chemical boffins) find themselves concurring with mind-body-spirit gurus who have for years said that the way you think – your attitude – can help you stay healthy or heal more quickly. You can benefit by by taking up meditation or yoga or listening to soothing music for relaxation. The result should be raised levels of beneficial natural body chemicals that boost immunity, and decreased levels of cortisol, a stress indicator.

58 | BE CANDID, LIKE POOH
THE TRUTH IS AN EFFECTIVE WEAPON

'That's right,' said Eeyore.
'Sing. Umty-tiddly, umty-too.
Here we go gathering Nuts and
May. Enjoy yourself.'
'I am,' said Pooh.

WINNIE-THE-POOH

EEYORE MAY BE speaking with irony or self-pity, but Pooh answers from the heart. Pooh is always candid, that is, he is frank (some might say blunt), sincere and invariably generous.

If you are willing to speak your thoughts aloud and be candid, especially with the truth, then you will have achieved a lot. However, few are so practised in the art as to attain the star status of Pooh. What is even more remarkable is that he has reached these stratospheric, meteoric heights yet remained unspoilt. Perhaps surprisingly, Pooh's whimsical language and frankness are an effective weapon. Sarcastic remarks and cynical ploys are dead in the water when they are hit full and square by an honest and sincere response. Try it one time.

But remember, when Pooh speaks the truth he does so thinking the best of everyone and he does not criticise unnecessarily in the name of being honest. This helps no one and can be hurtful.

'Can't you see?' shouted Piglet. 'Haven't you got eyes? Look at me!'

'I am looking, Roo, dear,' said Kanga rather severely. 'And you know what I told you yesterday about making faces. If you go on making faces like Piglet's, you will grow up to look like Piglet – and then think how sorry you will be. Now then, into the bath, and don't let me have to speak to you about it again.'

Before he knew where he was, Piglet was in the bath, and Kanga was scrubbing him firmly with a large lathery flannel.

WINNIE-THE-POOH

WHAT A BEAUTIFUL demonstration of how to have the last laugh! When Kanga realised that Piglet had been slipped into her pouch in place of Roo she decided, 'If they are having a joke with me, I will have a joke with them.' Kanga's virtuoso performance gave one of the perpetrators (namely Piglet) a taste of his own medicine. Her reaction was good-natured and it did not hurt anyone, apart from damping Piglet's dignity with a large soapy flannel. If you ever feel the need to pay someone back then perhaps you will consider this model of harmless fun as the way to do it.

'Here – we – are,' said Rabbit very slowly and carefully, 'all – of – us, and then, suddenly, we wake up one morning, and what do we find? We find a Strange Animal among us. An animal of whom we had never even heard before! An animal who carries her family about with her in her pocket!'

WINNIE-THE-POOH

RABBIT'S REACTION TO the arrival of Kanga and Roo is uncomfortable to witness because it smacks of discrimination against others for no reason other than their difference. Coupled with Rabbit's reaction to Tigger's bounciness, it also suggests intolerance.

It's important not to be too hasty in our judgement of others. Just because Kanga has a different lifestyle from some of the other animals it does not follow that she has different core values. She may be a single mother who carries her family in her pocket and bounds about instead of walking through the Forest. But as they get to know her, the other animals appreciate what a good mother she is and how loving and caring – she even adopts Tigger.

So while Rabbit is perhaps right to be initially cautious (rushing into new acquaintances can lead to difficulties of extrication at a later day), he'd be wise to wait and see how things develop before passing judgement.

. . . when you are a Bear of Very Little Brain, and you Think of Things, you find sometimes that a Thing which seemed very Thingish inside you is quite different when it gets out into the open and has other people looking at it.

THE HOUSE AT POOH CORNER

EVER WOKEN IN the night with a brilliant idea and written it down only to look at it in the cold light of day and realise it is, er, well . . . banal? If you haven't, you have the experience to look forward to, but most of us have asked a question at a public meeting or spoken an idea, or hastily sent an email or text message only to wish we could retract it immediately because the thought does not 'translate' into a convincing opinion or theory.

It takes courage to voice ideas so do not become despondent if people do not welcome yours immediately. Don't be afraid to speak out because hearing your suggestion 'out loud' may lead you to modify your idea into an even better one. Overcome your reticence at voicing your thoughts in front of others by regarding them as a sounding board – their comments and reactions will be helpful, just don't take them personally. After all, few great leaps forward are made by one person working in isolation. (It took several people using each other's observations to discover DNA.)

The media and literature are full of stories of authors, playwrights, inventors and others whose ideas were initially rejected, in some cases dozens of times, before they finally got their clockwork radios or see-through vacuum cleaners into production. So nurture your dreams even when they are received with a lack of enthusiasm by family, friends and colleagues. Keep on thinking and talking.

'And if anyone knows anything about anything,' said Bear to himself, 'it's Owl who knows something about something,' he said, 'or my name's not Winnie-the-Pooh,' he said. 'Which it is,' he added. 'So there you are.' Owl lived at The Chestnuts, an old-world residence of great charm, which was grander than anybody else's, or seemed so to Bear, because it had both a knocker and a bell-pull.

WINNIE-THE-POOH

OWL HAS CULTIVATED an aura of authoritative wisdom. He has all the trappings of success and a great deal of belief in his own knowledge and ability. He can cleverly bluff or blag his way through any sight-reading or spelling test. He is always ready and willing to give advice, even if he knows nothing about the subject. Naturally Pooh, who is trusting and respectful, consults Owl for advice and the benefit of his (questionable) wisdom. Well, in Pooh's situation, wouldn't you?

However, when seeking advice, be careful to whom you turn – it is hard to evaluate the quality of a person's counsel if you have no specialist knowledge in their area. That is the reason why it is best to consult a properly qualified expert, which is where professional organisations come in.

If they give you the wrong advice they should be indemnified by their insurance so you will have some recompense. Whether you want to learn to play the piano, borrow or invest money, take legal advice, have cosmetic surgery or try complementary medicine, find out the regulatory bodies for each profession or discipline and discover exactly what the letters after a person's name represent.

But be warned, some letters after experts' names are 'qualifications' earned after a weekend course – or less. They are about as valuable to you as Owl's olde worlde trappings and conventions – charming and attractive, but ultimately useless.

'It all comes,' said Rabbit sternly, 'of eating too *much*. I thought at the time,' said Rabbit, 'only I didn't like to say anything,' said Rabbit, 'that one of us was eating too much,' said Rabbit, 'and I knew it wasn't *me*,' he said . . . 'Then there's only one thing to be done,' he said. 'We shall have to wait for you to get thin again.'

'How long does getting thin take?' asked Pooh anxiously.

'About a week, I should think.' . . .

'A week!' said Pooh gloomily. 'What about meals?'

'I'm afraid no meals,' said Christopher Robin, 'because of getting thin quicker. But we *will* read to you.' . . .

'Then would you read a Sustaining Book, such as would help and comfort a Wedged Bear in Great Tightness?'

WINNIE-THE-POOH

POOH USED A crash diet once, in an emergency to get out of a particularly tight spot (Rabbit's front door), but it's not something he would want to do again – ever. And it is not something he would recommend. Neither do the world's leading nutrition and medical experts. As Pooh knows, diets don't work. Prevention is better.

Once you go back to your pre-dieting eating habits the weight returns. Crash diets (less than 800 calories a day) are a risk to health and do nothing to help re-educate eating patterns for an enjoyable life of tasty little somethings. The best way to lose weight permanently is to do it gradually. However, you have to want to lose weight to make it happen.

Reduce the amount you eat, improve the quality of your food and take more exercise. If you need to lose weight stay safe with a daily calorie intake of approximately 1,200 calories for women and 1,500 calories for men. This will allow safe weight loss, if necessary, at a rate of one to two pounds or a half to one kilogram per week. If these levels prove to be too high for you, reduce them by another 200 calories. And remember to be more active once you have lost weight.

'What?' said Piglet, with a jump. And then, to show that he hadn't been frightened, he jumped up and down once or twice more in an exercising sort of way.

WINNIE-THE-POOH

PIGLET HAS A tendency to be jumpy. Not surprising when you consider he is a small animal in a Forest where most animals are bigger, louder and bouncier than him. And although the example above, in which Piglet thinks he is in danger from a Woozle, is a genuinely stressful situation, he is often jumpy and stressed when he need not be.

We all need a certain amount of stress to help us meet deadlines and keep us alert, but equally we need to find ways of coping when the pressure is unremitting because cumulative pressure equals stress – the point at which we feel we cannot cope with the pressure at work, home or social situations. While stress will never go away entirely, we need to learn how to accept that it will be there and learn how to reduce it. Many people use watching TV, smoking and drinking alcohol to manage stress; others use exercise (walking, gym, jogging) and socialising (talking it through with friends). Some tactics are obviously better for us than others.

Learning how to think differently (remove the 'musts' and 'shoulds') is very helpful, as are other skills such as learning how to negotiate and accepting that anxiety is normal, it will pass and you can cope with it.

Relaxation techniques from tapes and books, regular exercise and setting realistic goals all help reduce stress.

Effective 'first aid' for stress includes breathing techniques, going for a walk, having a bath and listening to music or perhaps practising relaxing yoga poses or learning to meditate.

65 | PICK YOURSELF UP, DUST YOURSELF OFF AND COUNT YOUR BLESSINGS

Pooh had wandered into the Hundred Acre Wood, and was standing in front of what had once been Owl's House. It didn't look at all like a house now; it looked like a tree which had been blown down; and as soon as a house looks like that, it is time you tried to find another one.

THE HOUSE AT POOH CORNER

LIFE CAN BE (therefore it often is) punctuated by setbacks and false starts. That is life, so it's something we had better get used to, as our grandparents and great-grandparents did before us. Despite lower standards of living and lower incomes, only two per cent of people aged over sixty-five report suffering major depression during their lives, compared with fourteen per cent of today's thirty-five year olds with their higher incomes.

Could it be that living in a compensation-oriented culture we are less likely to pick ourselves up and dust ourselves off? Could it be that we are less likely to count our blessings and more likely to yearn for the things we do not have? Maybe media intrusion at personal, national and international disasters has the effect of making people linger on misfortune and pursue 'rights' instead of looking and moving forward. Imagine Owl with a microphone thrust in front of his face being asked, 'How do you feel now your home lies in ruins at your feet?' as he and the others surveyed the remains of the Wolery.

Owl lived in different times and the media circus did not whirl around him, so he and the others just got on with sorting the mess and finding him another home, Piglet's home – as it turned out (but that's another story of personal sacrifice and magnanimity on Piglet's part).

You don't have to be an optimist to overcome setbacks. In fact it is probably more helpful if you are slightly pessimistic or a pragmatist like Pooh and Piglet and, in this instance, Eeyore – who found Owl a new home.

'Tigger is all right, really,*' said Piglet lazily.
'Of course he is,' said Christopher Robin.
'Everybody is* really,*' said Pooh. 'That's
what* I *think,' said Pooh. 'But I don't
suppose I'm right,' he said.
'Of course you are,' said Christopher Robin.*

THE HOUSE AT POOH CORNER

THERE ARE TIMES when the (mis)behaviour of certain people makes you apoplectic with rage; you just want to . . . Well, you just want to! As Pooh observes, most people do not mean any harm. Even if they do, it's best not to let them make you angry, so before you confront them bring your anger under control. Counting to ten or taking some deep breaths is effective. Breathe slowly and deeply in through the nose and out fully through the mouth. Walking away from the scene before returning in a calmer state is a good idea, particularly if children are involved, because this will help prevent angry parents giving in to any urges to smack them.

As you walk away, scrunch your shoulders up to your ears, then let your shoulders fall away to release some of the tension you feel. When you are beginning to feel calmer and before dealing with the person who has angered you, if possible try standing in their shoes. See the world, or yourself, from where they are standing, and then you might feel differently about them. And if you don't? Go away and scream into a pillow.

For more deep-seated and long-held feelings of anger you need to learn to change the way you think, act and react. This may call for some help from a professional (a psychologist, maybe even a psychiatrist). Or investigate your beliefs and what triggers your moods. Try not to get angry – bottling up anger is one of the most common causes of headaches, according to scientists. Anger builds tension and tension builds headaches.

'. . . I can't swim. Bother!'
Then he had an idea, and I think that for a Bear of Very Little Brain, it was a good idea. He said to himself:
'If a bottle can float, then a jar can float, and if a jar floats, I can sit on the top of it, if it's a very big jar.'
So he took his biggest jar, and corked it up . . .
For a little while Pooh and The Floating Bear were uncertain as to which of them was meant to be on the top, but after trying one or two different positions, they settled down with The Floating Bear underneath and Pooh triumphantly astride it, paddling vigorously with his feet.

Winnie-the-Pooh

POOH'S 'BOAT' THE Floating Bear was launched after he made the basic 'scientific' (although he didn't realise it) observations described above.

It is said that necessity is the mother of invention, and when Pooh was faced with the necessity of taking a message in a bottle from Piglet – stranded in a flood – to someone who could read, he had to invent his boat. Having observed that the message floated to him in a bottle, Pooh rightly surmised that one of his empty honey jars, if corked, would also float. His prediction was proved to be correct when he put it into practice. Which suggests Pooh has something in common with Einstein who, you may recall, put his mind to the preoccupation of scientists of his day, to try to split the atom by bombarding it with energy. Einstein predicted that if it were split it would release untold masses of energy because, he surmised, that must be what was holding it together. It did and the result was the development of nuclear energy.

Like Pooh, Einstein followed through his simple thought to its logical conclusion. And that was just for starters. Later on he (Einstein, not Pooh) came up with the theory of relativity on which we base our ideas about the universe. Pooh continues to observe the universe with wonder. He has a ponder, then put his thoughts into practice – or verses.

Once upon a time, a very long time ago now, about last Friday, Winnie-the-Pooh lived in a forest all by himself under the name of Sanders.

WINNIE-THE-POOH

ARE YOU WHO you think you are? You probably were when you last looked but the trouble is, in uncertain times when the future is not assured, we often have to take on new roles and new jobs or change careers, so we may not be who we were when we started out. This can be very confusing, unless you accept that who you are is not fixed and final, in which case, it is less startling to have to reinvent yourself possibly several times, during your (working) life.

Sometimes your personal circumstances require you to question who you are and what you want to be. It may be that to earn a living you have to change roles. You may start out as an office assistant cum would-be film star, then find that the day job of a window cleaner is more lucrative (for the time being), and end up as a jeweller with a stall at a local craft market. Or there are other types of change in life with which you may not cope well, for example the change from an independent working life to one at home with babies and toddlers.

Many types of change can be disturbing and sometimes the difficulties are insoluble, but addressing them and making some adjustments *will* help.

If you feel that who or where you are at the moment is not who or where you want to be, start trying to work out what to do next. Keep a notebook and enter your current occupation, what you spend your time doing, how you habitually behave to yourself and others. Take time to observe others (no staring) and how they behave. Make a (surreptitious) note of the attractive and unattractive behaviours in others. Then list the less attractive aspects of yourself. Once you identify what you would like to change, try to write a realistic profile of who and what you would like to be. By this time you are part way to reinventing yourself. In extreme cases, it might mean changing friends and acquaintances and the way you dress and look or applying for retraining. But why not, if it's time for a change!

When Roo understood what he had to do, he was wildly excited, and cried out: 'Tigger, Tigger, we're going to jump! Look at me jumping, Tigger! Like flying, my jumping will be. Can Tiggers do it?' And he squeaked out: 'I'm coming, Christopher Robin!' and he jumped – straight into the middle of the tunic. And he was going so fast that he bounced up again almost as high as where he was before – and went on bouncing and saying, 'Oo!' for quite a long time – and then at last he stopped and said, 'Oo, lovely!'

THE HOUSE AT POOH CORNER

IF, AS AN adult, you have ever tried to learn to ski or to parachute, or do something equally challenging, then it's likely you will have shared Tigger's fears as he stood at the top of the tree preparing to jump into Christopher Robin's outstretched tunic. It is very unlikely that you will have embraced the rescue leap with the enthusiasm and trust that Roo shows. Now, you might say that is because Roo is young and he does not realise the danger he is facing. Or you might say that Roo has no fear because he has not yet learned to feel it.

Roo is free from all the psychological fears and inhibitions that get in the way of adults – and adolescents – trying to learn to ski, or jump from parachutes, or take up salsa dancing at which they may look stupid or undignified before becoming accomplished performers. Of course, you may not want to learn to ski or to take up sky diving; if that is the case do not be forced (persuaded or bullied) into doing something that you have no wish or need to do.

However, if you really do want to do something that scares you, it makes sense to try to abandon some of your fear (while taking adequate safety precautions). Embrace what you do with enthusiasm, then you will no doubt be more successful. People who are open to new challenges in a relaxed state of awareness, are far less likely to fail or fall and break a leg on the ski slopes than those in a tense, fearful state for whom you can predict self-fulfilling accidents and failure. Face up to your fears, try to assess logically how realistic they are, then do it anyway.

'Could you fly up to the letter-box with Piglet on your back?' he asked.
'No,' said Piglet quickly. 'He couldn't.'
Owl explained about the Necessary Dorsal Muscles. He had explained this to Pooh and Christopher Robin once before, and had been waiting ever since for a chance to do it again, because it is a thing which you can easily explain twice before anybody knows what you are talking about.

THE HOUSE AT POOH CORNER

THE VERY IDEA of taking physical exercise would, I suspect, seem preposterous to Owl, although I have never raised the matter with him (I wouldn't dare). Perspiration, huffing and puffing, Lycra shorts and getting wet in the showers would be . . . indignity beyond endurance, either in public or in private. Yet flying requires the necessary dorsal muscles to be toned. Winnie-the-Pooh's triceps similarly need to be toned to ease him from the armchair, and his biceps need to be capable of lifting heavy honey pots.

So if, like Bear and Owl, you are far too dignified to be seen at a public gymnasium or an exercise class, then you need to invest in other ways to stay fit. Consider videotapes of a routine that suits your needs, or an instruction manual by a qualified teacher. You can even exercise from your armchair or at your desk. Here's one for a flat stomach to do now. Sit up straight in your chair, lean forward slightly, placing hands on thighs. Take a deep breath in through the nose. Breathing out through the mouth, pull the tummy muscles in tightly (imagine you are trying to get your navel to touch your spine). Hold for a few seconds, breathing normally.

Relax and take another breath in through the nostrils. Breathe out through the mouth and repeat, pulling in the tummy muscles. Do this exercise five times to start with, increasing repetitions to suit your needs.

*He
climbed
and
he
climbed
and
he
climbed,
and
as
he
climbed
he
sang
a
little
song
to
himself.*

WINNIE-THE-POOH

POOH IS FULL of ambition to reach the top of the tree, which to him is like the end of the rainbow where there is a pot of gold (honey) to be found. Drawn onwards and upwards by the buzzing of the bees, Pooh is convinced that there will be nectar . . . ambrosia . . . all the delights of an overflowing honey pot just as soon as he reaches the top. His is a solitary climb but most of us meet others on our way up the ladder of life. Pooh sings a happy little ditty as he goes on his way, and we too would do well to be cheerful and pleasant to those we pass on the way. View it as an investment of sorts: be nice to people on the way up because you never know who you are going to meet on the way down. One day you may be applying for a job from the trainee you helped reach the next rung of the ladder. As long as you did not bully or humiliate him or her and you shared some of your wisdom, he or she should be well disposed towards you.

He [Pooh] hurried back to his own house; and his mind was so busy on the way with the hum that he was getting ready for Eeyore that, when he suddenly saw Piglet sitting in his best arm-chair, he could only stand there rubbing his head and wondering whose house he was in.
'Hallo, Piglet,' he said. 'I thought you were out.'
'No,' said Piglet, 'it's you who were out, Pooh.'
'So it was,' said Pooh. 'I knew one of us was.'

THE HOUSE AT POOH CORNER

HAVE YOU EVER travelled somewhere and realised, horrified, on arrival that you do not remember the journey there? Or paid for your shopping then left it, or your credit card, at the shop? If you have, you will relate to Pooh's mindlessness (above). It's that feeling of not being fully present even when you are physically there.

While operating on one level in a mindless state, Pooh is also being 'mindful'. In the case above he is walking home mechanically without thinking about the journey while mindfully composing a Hum to share with Eeyore (since Piglet was not at home to hear it). While Pooh's episode of mindlessness is harmless to him and others, there is a danger that if we habitually live in a mindless state we will see, and experience, what we expect, and not what is actually happening. If you live in this state you are in danger of missing much of what is going on around you. You could have much more fun in life if you lived more in the present. If you experience every event (every drive to work, every trip to the grocery store) more in the present, then you will become more aware and livelier and a more reliable witness. If you really look around you, if you really notice what is happening, if you approach everything as if it is the first time you have done it, then you are less likely to become cynical, and jaded and to adopt the tired attitude 'Been there, done that'. By experiencing every day as a new day and being in-the-moment you will be putting into practice part of Pooh's approach to life.

*'Look, Pooh!' said Piglet suddenly.
'There's something in one of the
Pine Trees.'
'So there is!' said Pooh, looking up
wonderingly. 'There's an Animal.'
Piglet took Pooh's arm, in case
Pooh was frightened.*

THE HOUSE AT POOH CORNER

MOTHERS INSTINCTIVELY cuddle babies and small children to comfort them when they cry, fall over or are upset. When a child has a tummy ache they often guide a parent's hand to the spot that hurts and a gentle rub can bring some relief.

We hug our partners and family and friends as a sign of affection, and when we want to congratulate or commiserate, we hug. We do it because it has a very positive effect. It's as though an invisible energy source passes between us so that we 'recharge' each other's batteries through touch. Sometimes a simple touch that is not as all-embracing as a hug can also act to defuse tension in a conversation. In other circumstances, a light touch on the arm during a conversation builds a bond, creating a feeling of enhanced intimacy. Although we hardly need scientific proof to convince us of the benefits and the healing power of touch, it exists. MRI scans of the brain reveal that when we are stroked or touched nerves in the skin transmit messages to the brain to trigger pleasant emotional responses.

This brings new meaning to the common or garden injunction to our friends to keep in touch. Perhaps we should try being more tactile, where appropriate, and less shy about giving people, especially those who we know to be lonely, a hug.

'*What do you think, Christopher Robin?*' asked Eeyore a little anxiously, feeling that something wasn't quite right.
Christopher Robin had a question to ask first, and he was wondering how to ask it.
'Well,' he said at last, 'it's a very nice house, and if your own house is blown down, *you* must go somewhere else, mustn't you, Piglet? What would *you* do, if your *house was blown down?*'
Before Piglet could think, Pooh answered for him.
'He'd come and live with me,' said Pooh, 'wouldn't you, Piglet?'

THE HOUSE AT POOH CORNER

THAT'S WHAT FRIENDS are for – providing support when you need it, from a roof over your head to a sympathetic ear and a shoulder to cry on. So do you really need to spend the morning with a Jungian therapist probing your conscious for an hour a day, five days a week for several years, or having full-blown Freudian psychoanalysis of your unconscious?

Well, it doesn't seem to matter whether you do or you don't, because what it comes down to in the end is that all of them probably work equally well for the people whom they are going to benefit (which is not everyone). And that if you have psychological problems (as opposed to clinical depression or psychiatric problems), you would do just as well talking to any of your friends who are capable of encouraging you and activating hope.

Practical advice from a reliable, intelligent and understanding friend, if you are lucky enough to have one, is likely to be just as good as advice from an accredited counsellor.

'Where are we going?' said Pooh . . .
'Nowhere,' said Christopher Robin.
So they began going there, and after
they had walked a little way
Christopher Robin said: 'What do you
like doing best in the world, Pooh?'
'Well,' said Pooh, 'what I like best –'
' . . . what I like doing best is
Nothing,' [said Christopher Robin].
'How do you do Nothing?' asked
Pooh, after he had wondered for a
long time.
'Well, it's when people call out at you
just as you're going off to do it,
"What are you going to do,
Christopher Robin?" and you say
"Oh, nothing," and then you go and
do it . . . It means just going along,
listening to all the things you can't
hear, and not bothering.'

THE HOUSE AT POOH CORNER

WITH ONE FOOT in the world of childhood and one foot in the world of school, learning and growing up, Christopher Robin is about to leave the childhood Utopia of living in the moment and join the headlong rush to 'get there' (school, exams, work, meetings, hobbies) on time. It's reassuring to know that Pooh will always Be There for him when he finds time to Do Nothing.

Doing Nothing from time to time on a regular basis, or finding time to stand and stare, is something that will benefit us all. Among the benefits of Doing Nothing are that it . . .

● Enables your brain to go 'offline' and 'think'.

● Slows your heart rate and lowers your blood pressure.

● Can boost immunity. Relaxation suppresses the release of stress-related hormones that depress the immune system.

● Improves digestion. Stress hormones can increase stomach acidity, causing indigestion and destroying beneficial gut bacteria that protect against constipation, stomach upsets – even some cancers.

● Improves concentration and boosts creative thinking. Deep relaxation and meditation are, strictly speaking, proactive. They can change brain-waves, thought processes and brain function.

● Eases pain and tiredness. Lying down in a darkened room helps headaches and it can relieve any pressure on joints.

All of which means there is a lot of potential benefit to be gained from joining Pooh and Christopher Robin in doing the least taxing activity you can think of – nothing!

Then he [Pooh] began to think of all the things Christopher Robin would want to tell him when he came back from wherever he was going to, and how muddling it would be for a Bear of Very Little Brain to try and get them right in his mind.

THE HOUSE AT POOH CORNER

IT IS NOT that Pooh is bad at clear thinking or that he can't do it, it is just that he has not yet learned the skill. Learning (which is what Christopher Robin is going off to school to do) involves receiving information, memorising it, processing the information to understand it and then communicating or applying the knowledge. A simple explanation, but adequate for us to understand how Pooh could clear the muddle in his mind. When Christopher Robin tells him things, he could make notes – writing something down helps us memorise it and aids recall. In the same way, if we want to work out something that is puzzling or muddling us we can jot it down on paper, for example to sort out the pros and cons of a situation (new job, moving home, choosing a particular holiday). Some brain experts recommend abandoning standard linear notes (writing out sentences) in favour of noting only key words and using different colours and linking words and ideas to make 'mind maps' of your notes. For people whose brains find it easier to learn non-verbally, this method may be easier. The key word (whether it is a thought or piece of information) sits in the centre of the page and further information or thoughts radiate from the centre along linking lines. These in turn have branches for subsidiary information and thoughts. The diagrams end up looking like spiders or childlike drawings of the sun. It's a useful device that might help Pooh, and you, sort out any muddling thoughts or learn some new things.

'Nobody tells me,' said Eeyore. 'Nobody keeps me informed. I make it seventeen days come Friday since anybody spoke to me.'
'It certainly isn't seventeen days . . . I was here myself a week ago.'
'Not conversing,' said Eeyore. 'Not first one and then the other. You said "Hallo" and Flashed Past. I saw your tail a hundred yards up the hill as I was meditating my reply. I had thought of saying "What?" – but, of course, it was then too late.'
'Well, I was in a hurry.'

THE HOUSE AT POOH CORNER

HOW OFTEN HAVE you heard or used being in a hurry as an excuse for not stopping or not passing the time? It is very easy to do. If we are in a constant rush we are in danger of being so busy that we will miss the important events – and thoughts and concerns – of those who are near and dear to us.

Finding time for a meaningful conversation – more than just an exchange of 'Hello' or 'How are you?' – makes us connect with people and places. If you (and your partner) pass like proverbial ships in the night then your relationship is in danger of running aground or being fatally holed. If you do not listen carefully to what those close to you are saying then you are only there in person and do not meet their emotional needs. Don't think they don't notice. They do, even if they don't themselves understand or articulate their feeling of loss. Even if they find a form of words, like Eeyore, you might be long gone before they can express it to you. Before you know it they will have grown up, left home, moved away – or died! So keep talking, take part in their battles and indulge in a few happy family conflicts. In the same way, keep in touch with the grassroots where you live or in the blink of an eye your local rainforest will be chopped down, there will be a motorway running through your front garden, or your neighbourhood library will have closed when your name on the petition could have made all the difference. Once communication breaks down families fall apart, civilisations fall and empires are lost!

'I suppose none of you are sitting on a thistle by any chance?'

'I believe I am,' said Pooh. 'Ow!' He got up, and looked behind him. 'Yes, I was. I thought so.'

'Thank you, Pooh. If you've quite finished with it.' He moved across to Pooh's place, and began to eat.

'It doesn't do them any Good, you know, sitting on them,' he went on as he looked up munching.

'Takes all the Life out of them. Remember that another time, all of you. A little Consideration, a little Thought for Others, makes all the difference.'

WINNIE-THE-POOH

IT IS INDEED very inconsiderate to sit on another person's packed lunch and Pooh most certainly would not have sat on Eeyore's lunch if he had recognised it as a meal. It is also a little unfair of Eeyore to berate everyone about being thoughtless when they may well have been unaware of Eeyore's custom of eating prickly plants. However, Eeyore does have a point. We should make ourselves aware of the customs and habits of others and respect those customs and practices. While we are generally aware of what offends and what is acceptable in our own backyard, we need to make sure that we know how to conduct ourselves beyond our own street, county, country and religion. That way we will minimise the likelihood of diplomatic or international incidents caused by sitting on someone else's sandwiches.

Christopher Robin came down from the Forest to the bridge, feeling all sunny and careless, and just as if twice nineteen didn't matter a bit, as it didn't on such a happy afternoon, and he thought that if he stood on the bottom rail of the bridge, and leant over, and watched the river slipping slowly away beneath him, then he would suddenly know everything there was to be known, and he would be able to tell Pooh, who wasn't quite sure about some of it.

THE HOUSE AT POOH CORNER

LIKE MANY PEOPLE, Christopher Robin and Pooh share a vague feeling that there is a question to which they need an answer, if only they could think of the question. It is, of course, the one that surfaces in everyone's mind at one time or another – the one about the Meaning of Life, the Universe and Everything. But on such a sunny afternoon in a sunny childhood Christopher Robin is only dimly aware of a dawning realisation that he might wish to ask this question. Even so he is drawn to the water's edge to watch time slip away while his consciousness changes gear from the classroom to a state of deep relaxation. Of course he does not realise he is in a transcendental state of mind and, sadly, it's a knack we lose with adult experience. However, we can rediscover it and lose our sense of self through meditation or prayer. A healthy spiritual life contributes to greater resistance to illness, and a longer and happier life. But it's likely you will only benefit from prayer if you have genuine religious faith. And like learning to meditate, prayer takes practice. You have to work at it to get in touch with the essence of yourself. It probably won't work if you only say a prayer when you are in an emergency.

For people who, like Pooh, are more pragmatic the meaning in life is more likely to be found by helping others.

It may be that you will never find an answer to the question 'What is the meaning of life?' But if you don't start looking you will never know.

'Oh, Eeyore,' began Piglet a little nervously, because Eeyore was busy.
Eeyore put out a paw and waved him away.
'To-morrow,' said Eeyore. 'Or the next day.' . . .
'Oh, Eeyore,' he began again, 'I just –'
'Is that little Piglet?' said Eeyore, still looking hard at his sticks.
'Yes, Eeyore, and I –'
'Do you know what this is?'
'No,' said Piglet.
'It's an A.'
'Oh,' said Piglet.
'Not O – A,' said Eeyore severely. 'Can't you hear, or do you think you have more education than Christopher Robin?'
'Yes,' said Piglet. 'No,' said Piglet very quickly. And he came closer still.
'Christopher Robin said it was an A, and an A it is – until somebody treads on it,' Eeyore added sternly.
'Piglet jumped backwards hurriedly . . .

THE HOUSE AT POOH CORNER

ONCE AGAIN PIGLET has not been able to communicate his feelings or his need for an explanation because he is not assertive enough. If Piglet were more assertive he would be able to influence Eeyore and point out (to Eeyore) the negative effect Eeyore's behaviour and attitude was having on him (Piglet). He would also be able to more quickly assimilate what Eeyore is talking about. Being more assertive would boost Piglet's self-confidence and he would feel less anxious about Heffalumps, bouncy Tiggers and his other worries.

And the same applies to us. We all need to assert ourselves to be able to work well with others and be more effective as a team member and an individual. If we are assertive we are able to communicate our needs, wants and feelings and that will make life pleasanter at home and at work. Ideally, we want to do that without denying others their wants or needs, but being assertive means being able to negotiate in a calm and controlled way so that if necessary a compromise is arrived at.

There may be many reasons why we are not assertive, for example up-bringing, schooling, bullying at work –

but whatever the reason, we can learn to change our behaviour.

Incidentally, being assertive does not mean being aggressive (shouting, finger-stabbing, threatening language – 'You'd better, or else . . .') It means expressing your true feelings and opinions clearly and honestly to people's faces. At times it might mean being a little bit 'difficult' in the nicest possible way. But you are in good company, because being difficult (in the sense of assertive) can be done politely and firmly, as Pooh shows when he says 'No' to Owl sharing his birthday present for Eeyore.

'Hallo, Eeyore,' they called out cheerfully.

'Ah!' said Eeyore. 'Lost your way?'

'We just came to see you,' said Piglet. 'And to see how your house was. Look, Pooh, it's still standing!'

'I know,' said Eeyore. 'Very odd. Somebody ought to have come down and pushed it over.'

'We wondered whether the wind would blow it down,' said Pooh.

'Ah, that's why nobody's bothered, I suppose. I thought perhaps they'd forgotten.'

'Well, we're very glad to see you, Eeyore, and now we're going on to see Owl.'

'That's right. You'll like Owl. He flew past a day or two ago and noticed me. He didn't actually say anything, mind you, but he knew it was me. Very friendly of him, I thought. Encouraging.'

Pooh and Piglet shuffled about a little and said, 'Well, good-bye, Eeyore,' as lingeringly as they could, but they had a long way to go, and wanted to be getting on.

THE HOUSE AT POOH CORNER

THERE ARE SOME people, like Eeyore, whose negativity literally drains you of energy. They take but they give nothing in return. They want answers to their problems and talk only about themselves, showing, at best, only a perfunctory interest in you. Others are so tense and stressed you feel wound up before they even begin to unburden themselves. Somehow their tension rubs off on you. Others are so earnest and serious that there is no room for spontaneous enjoyment of the time spent with them. And some seem to be lacking a sense of humour or to have had an irony bypass. Still others just want to show off and crow about their achievements and successes, sometimes only to highlight areas in which you have not been so successful or in which they perceive you to be deficient.

These people can never be considered true friends. They are the persistent offenders that you come across through family ties or work commitments or because you have the misfortune to live next door to them. These people differ from your true friends who, when they are going through a rough patch in their lives, need your support. Friends, like Eeyore, can be helped out of their bad moods with just a little input. Eeyore was 'bounced' out of himself and into a little gaiety and jollity when there were little cakes with pink icing to be shared. And he does try to find Small and help rescue Roo.

No, the people we are talking about avoiding are insufferable bores and they do not deserve your time. You are going to have to make the decision to drop them from your circle of 'friends' – and act on that decision – or spend the minimum amount of time you can with them.

> *'We had breakfast together yesterday. By the Pine Trees. I'd made up a little basket, just a little, fair-sized basket, an ordinary biggish sort of basket, full of – '*
>
> THE HOUSE AT POOH CORNER

JUST AS ONE man's meat is another man's poison, so one bear's ordinary sort of portion is a Piglet's supply of food for a month. Portion control is something that 'flexible eaters' who do not have a weight problem do automatically. If, for example, they eat a large lunch, they have only a small snack – a haycorn or two – for supper. If they party one day on cakes with pink icing and other indulgences, they eat less (possibly without realising or making a fuss about it) over the ensuing days. This balances out their calorie intake over time and prevents weight gain.

Portion size has been identified by international obesity experts as a major cause of weight gain in the developed world. 'Whopper' and 'king-size' portions, 'meal deals' and 'super-size' confectionery items, together with financial incentives to 'buy one and get one free', are fuelling obesity. It is all very difficult to resist, especially since high-calorie fast foods are so readily available. Couple availability with the natural tendency for most people to be a 'plate cleaner' and it is a recipe for weight gain.

Experiments show that when given free meals the majority of people eat it all up whether it is a 1,000-gram or a 500-gram portion. Yet afterwards they report hunger being equally satisfied by the moderate portion. However, when 'flexible eaters' choose a large portion they adjust their intake later, or leave some food.

Flexible eaters seem capable of holding back some of the time and relaxing at other times without going to the extremes of dieting or bingeing. You might like to try to follow their example, but until that behaviour comes naturally you may have to adopt the maxim 'Stop, Think' (Am I really hungry? Do I really need this?) before you put food in your mouth. Or maybe you are thirsty and a glass of water would do just as well as another ordinary, biggish slice of Victoria Sponge. Although Pooh, no doubt, would say, 'Couldn't I have both?'

'Many happy returns of Eeyore's birthday,' said Pooh.
'Oh, is that what it is?'
'What are you giving him, Owl?'
'What are you giving him, Pooh?'
'I'm giving him a Useful Pot to Keep Things In, and I wanted to ask you –' . . .
'You ought to write "A Happy Birthday" on it.'
'That was what I wanted to ask you,' said Pooh . . .
'It's a nice pot,' said Owl, looking at it all round.
'Couldn't I give it too? From both of us?'
'No,' said Pooh. 'That would not be a good plan.'

WINNIE-THE-POOH

THAT IS THE second time Pooh has had to say 'No' about sharing his birthday gift to Eeyore. First Piglet asked, 'Couldn't I give it too? From both of us?' and now Owl is asking the same favour. Pooh gently refuses, not from selfish motives, but so that Eeyore might receive more gifts and attention.

We teach children to say 'No' to strangers and to unsafe demands on them, but we are not as good about saying 'No' ourselves. It takes practice to take on only what you know you can achieve, or what you want to do, and to say 'No' politely but firmly to the rest. Of course, it's easy to say 'No' if you are in mortal danger, as Tigger felt when he was stuck up the pine tree with Roo. On that occasion he could say 'No' to going to the top of the tree, 'No' to falling off the branch and 'No' to eating the sandwiches (mainly because they were at the bottom of the tree). In real life, even when we are put in a dangerous position, such as being given a lift in a car by someone we know to have been drinking alcohol, it can be difficult to say 'No'.

In less difficult circumstances, it can be all too easy to be caught out by a seemingly innocuous or casual request.

There are many circumstances in which you have to say 'No', but in the main the most important refusals are those that over-burden you. After all, you will be the one who becomes run down and over-tired and whose health and well-being will be at risk, not the person who asked you to take on the task. 'Not a good plan,' as Pooh says.

The power of saying 'No' can be life-transforming, from helping to lose weight to giving up smoking or saying 'No' to a job you have been doing for so long you thought you would never change . . .

'Many happy returns of the day,' called out Pooh, forgetting that he had said it already.
'Thank you, Pooh, I'm having them,' said Eeyore gloomily.
'I've brought you a little present,' said Pooh excitedly . . .
'It's a Useful Pot,' said Pooh . . . 'And it's for putting things in. There!'
When Eeyore saw the pot, he became quite excited.
'Why!' he said. 'I believe my Balloon will just go into that Pot!' . . .
'I'm very glad,' said Pooh happily, 'that I thought of giving you a Useful Pot to put things in.'
'I'm very glad,' said Piglet happily, 'that I thought of giving you Something to put in a Useful Pot.'
But Eeyore wasn't listening. He was taking the balloon out, and putting it back again, as happy as could be . . .

WINNIE-THE-POOH

IT MAY BE regarded as a cliché, and it is probably also a truism, that money cannot buy or guarantee happiness. Even though Pooh ate the honey he was planning to give Eeyore for his birthday and had to give him the empty pot instead, and even though Piglet tripped and burst the balloon, presenting Eeyore with a small piece of damp rag, Eeyore was happy with these gifts, perhaps proving another cliché, that it is The Thought That Counts, rather than the value of the gift.

Of course, money is vital to satisfy our basic needs for food, water, shelter and warmth and for safety, security and stability in our lives, but there are more important contributors to happiness. We need to give and receive love from family and friends and have self-esteem, respect or recognition. Only when these needs have been met are we able to be creative and have the luxury of pursuing interests that give us Personal Fulfilment. What we don't need is 'stuff'.

Too much 'stuff', or money to buy 'stuff', does not make us happy. Even misers and misanthropes who hoard money remain discontented. Eeyore, however, is delighted with his empty honey pot and broken balloon because he has the imagination to play with them, just as children can have as much fun playing with an empty cardboard box as they can with certain expensive toys.

Some people who have experienced the rare phenomenon of a change of circumstances that takes them from rags to riches reflect that when they had nothing they were happier because they had their family or a strong sense of belonging to a community. Everyone was equally poor but made their fun together.

Once we know that beyond a certain point money will not make us happy or happier, we can relax and stop craving a faster car or bigger house or more exotic holidays. In giving up that grasping for more we give up the unhappiness that accompanies it. Instead we can pursue self-development and creativity.

85 | IS THERE ANYBODY THERE?

> *'Is anybody at home?'*
> *There was a sudden scuffling noise from inside the hole, and then silence.*
> *'What I said was, "Is anybody at home?"' called out Pooh very loudly.*
> *'No,' said a voice; and then added, 'You needn't shout so loud. I heard you quite well the first time.'*
> *'Bother!' said Pooh. 'Isn't there anybody here at all?'*
> *'Nobody.'*
>
> WINNIE-THE-POOH

HOME TELEPHONE, WORK telephone, mobile telephone, email, fax, letters – there are so many demands on your time that have the potential to increase stress and encroach on personal and family space that you need to limit your responses. This must be how Rabbit felt.

Don't answer every call on your time every time (obviously don't ignore the important ones, and the brown envelopes containing bills) but let some issues ride or float for a while. If the issue really matters the caller will persist (but be aware that some persistent ones are also the ones that are unimportant or a waste of your time). Become more discriminating in your responses. This does not mean you need to be impolite or unpleasant, just decline politely but firmly.

And finally, if you decide to ignore the phone then do ignore it – don't make a half-hearted or bungled attempt at it, like Rabbit. Switch on the answer phone if you have one and turn the ringer volume down or off, switch off your mobile and just ignore them for a while when you need to.

'I'm not saying there won't be an Accident now, mind you. They're funny things, Accidents. You never have them till you're having them.'

THE HOUSE AT POOH CORNER

THERE'S LITTLE DOUBT that Eeyore would have made an excellent Boy Scout and he would probably have graduated to Scout Leader. His attitude to life is that it is an enormous risk so one had better expect the worst and Be Prepared.

Eeyore would undoubtedly take all necessary precautions and be prepared for all eventualities. He would know what to say to a Heffalump (unlike Piglet), he would take provisions on an expotition – or devise a route that ensured a plentiful supply of thistles. Eeyore would be that nagging grown-up voice during childhood that variously warned you to: Be Careful, Look both ways before crossing the road, Do not sit on wet grass, Never go out without a clean handkerchief, Carry a spare pair of pants in your bag along with a survival blanket and enough food to last five days on an open mountain side (in case of accidents), Always wear a vest unless there is an R in the month, Avoid drinking out of wet glasses, Never play with matches, Never loiter near an open fire in flammable nightwear . . . and so on.

You will have realised by now that the above are reasonable precautions mixed with a smattering of superstition and the ramblings of an old grey donkey who regards life as a disease or risk that is best avoided. It is not. Avoiding accidents is about taking reasonable precautions such as following the *Highway Code*, signalling your intentions and taking out adequate insurance – and having done that, enjoying yourself.

If you took everything you read or heard about accidents seriously you would never go out of your home. You would certainly not venture into the garden since even gardening has been declared a 'danger sport'. One in five of all domestic injuries and one in seventy-five of domestic fatalities occurs in or around the garden (think ladders, power tools). Similarly, you would never wear an anorak (and not for sartorial reasons). A major UK hospital has found a link between wearing an anorak with the hood up and injury from road traffic accidents because they more than halve your field of vision. This leads us to conclude that while life may be an accident waiting to happen, it's up to us whether we join in the game or stand sadly on the sidelines like Eeyore.

27 | DON'T TRY TOO HARD – LET THINGS HAPPEN

'And that's the whole poem,' he said.
'Do you like it, Piglet?'
'All except the shillings,' said Piglet.
'I don't think they ought to be there.'
'They wanted to come in after the pounds,'
explained Pooh, 'so I let them. It is the best
way to write poetry, letting things come.'
'Oh, I didn't know,' said Piglet.

THE HOUSE AT POOH CORNER

IT'S QUITE SIMPLE when Pooh explains it: you don't write poetry, it comes to you. Like many things in life, you can relax and let it happen, ergo the wildlife garden, or you can cultivate, titivate and force nature to follow your garden design plan. The best results usually lie somewhere between the two. So you need to make some effort, but not strain to produce something contrived. Which means you need balance in your life.

Achieving a balance between working lives (whether that is a paid-for job, or being a parent or carer) and home and personal lives is an on-going challenge for many of us. Consider what would make the balance better for you – probably having more control of your working life.

Key questions to ask yourself (and answer) are: what are you passionate about, what motivates and inspires you, what are your strengths and what is your purpose in life? Big questions, I know, but answering them will enable you to set goals and give you a focus. But don't try too hard – leave the questions at the back of your mind and let the answers come to you.

'It all comes, I suppose,' he decided, as he said good-bye to the last branch, spun round three times, and flew gracefully into a gorse-bush, 'it all comes of liking honey so much. Oh, help!'

WINNIE-THE-POOH

AS YOU ARE aware, Pooh plummeted out of a tree after climbing it in search of honey: when we go to unreasonable ends to gratify our particular pleasures, we risk coming unstuck or unhinged! The old adage is true when it recommends moderation in all things. We usually take this to refer to eating and drinking (alcohol), but it can also be applied to gambling, sloth, greed, honey, thistles, haycorns and other assorted 'sins'. There can, however, be no moderation in smoking and recreational drugs because any amount is potentially deadly.

We speak of being 'addicted' to tea and coffee and some of us describe ourselves as chocoholics because we love chocolate and probably eat more than is good for us. But these are minor problems because you cannot be addicted to chocolate or coffee – it's a state of mind not a physiological addiction. Similarly, you might be a habitual user of swear words, but you are not addicted to swearing, and your behaviour can be changed. Yet how do you recognise the danger signs when you might be having too much of a thing that is not very good for you?

It might sound obvious, but the symptoms can go unnoticed – strong desire or compulsion to take the substance, an inability to stop yourself, increased tolerance of the substance or activity, pre-occupation with using or doing it and persistent use. There are genetic predispositions to behaviour that leads to addiction or dependence on alcohol or pills or gambling – or even shopping and excessive eating – but the arguments continue about whether addiction can be seen entirely as a medical issue without any moral responsibility and whether genes directly 'cause' addiction or the type of personality that cannot do anything in moderation.

Among those working with addicts, there is a belief that whatever the personality or genes, you ultimately have responsibility for what you are doing and you can stop if you want to. But you have to decide that it is what you really want to do. That doesn't mean it is easy to do (it's notoriously difficult) but you can do it.

The Old Grey Donkey, Eeyore, stood by himself in a thistly corner of the Forest, his front feet well apart, his head on one side, and thought about things. Sometimes he thought sadly to himself, 'Why?' and sometimes he thought, 'Wherefore?' and sometimes he thought, 'Inasmuch as which?' – and sometimes he didn't quite know what he was thinking about.

WINNIE-THE-POOH

AT THIS POINT Eeyore has either reached a blissful meditative state, or it's time for him, and us, to learn a little about how to free up the mind and allow ourselves to stop worrying (thinking about ourselves and what is happening around us) and meditate.

At the first attempt, it's likely you'll spend the time fidgeting and thinking about what you 'should' be doing. From then on it's a question of practice. The ideal is to set a regular time to meditate for ten minutes once or twice a day. You can do the incense and candles bit and create a sacred space in the privacy of your home; equally you can get to work ten minutes earlier and do it at your desk (ignoring phones and so on) before everyone else arrives. The important thing is that meditation is a regular quiet time to yourself.

Lotus position (cross-legged on the floor with palms upturned resting on knees and forefinger and thumb closed in a circle) is not compulsory. You can lie down if you like (but stay awake) or sit up straight with hands on thighs and feet on the ground. You might also need to do some quick exercises to release tension in the neck and head before starting your meditation, for example, hunching shoulders to ears a few times and

rolling the head gently or clenching and releasing facial or other muscles.

At first, establishing a regular rhythm of breathing to help the mind settle might mean counting 4–2–4–2, inhaling for four, breathing out for two, and so on until you do it automatically.

Humming a mantra (simple sound) like 'om' is not compulsory, but some people find it helps to focus on a sound – or an object, such as a vase of flowers or the fruit bowl. Once focussed, the aim is to enter a deep state of relaxation and awareness. This is called passive meditating. It is not the same as 'relaxing' in front of the TV with a glass of Chardonnay. Meditation produces peace of mind and a sense of detachment from the pressures of life and has a longer-lasting effect. Active meditation is when you can practise meditation while walking around or getting on with other things. You can learn from books, tapes and lessons – tapes are especially good.

It may take some years (or decades even) to emit the calm, serenity and happiness typified by the transcendental smile on the Buddha's face, but with practice you may reach nirvana. Indeed, scientists have measured the brain-waves of practising Buddhists and found the part of the brain associated with positive emotions and good moods is unusually active among them.

Meditation can also slow heart rate, lower blood pressure and alter brainwaves, proving that a meditative state exists and that it has bodily effects.

Although there is no incontrovertible proof that meditation benefits health it seems to help some people control stress and to a small degree it may benefit some asthma and epilepsy sufferers and help pain control.

Anything that has the potential to lift Eeyore out of his gloom towards a more transcendental state of mind is worth a try.

'But this is Me!' said Bear, very much surprised.
'What sort of Me?'
'Pooh Bear.'
'Are you sure?' said Rabbit, still more surprised.
'Quite, quite sure,' said Pooh.

WINNIE-THE-POOH

NOT EVERYONE IS as confident about who they are as Pooh, and that can lead to problems. Fixing your identity, knowing who you are, and working within your capabilities while stretching yourself to meet new challenges defines who you are. But how do you know who you are? Often the answer is reflected back at you in the way you are perceived by others. To some you may appear successful and confident, which can make them talk about you behind your back and gossip about you either in a jealous or an admiring tone! To others, you are of more interest when things are going badly for you and they can talk about what does not work in their lives, commiserate, and feel that perhaps you are worse off than them. It could be that you find you have chameleon tendencies – you make your life appear better or worse to fit the mood or expectations of your friends or work colleagues. You might be hiding your capabilities and putting yourself down and minimising your ability. Perhaps it is time to stop placing importance on what others think and decide what you really want to do in your life. Focus on what you are good at and work at being even better at it to realise your full potential so that you once again feel connected to what matters to you.

Focus on your strengths – the things others like about you, the things you do well, problems you have handled well, things you are glad you do, compliments paid to you. Identify the situations in which you are at your best, then work towards change that will see you operating in an area that better suits your ability. And work towards communicating who you are and what matters to you to your friends and acquaintances. It is not the easy way out, but it should put you on course to greater confidence and being more at ease with yourself.

| # Everybody Needs a Holiday in Which to Piece Themselves Back Together

'And how are you?' said Winnie-the-Pooh.
Eeyore shook his head from side to side.
'Not very how,' he said. 'I don't seem to have
felt at all how for a long time.'
'Dear, dear,' said Pooh, 'I'm sorry about that.
Let's have a look at you.'

WINNIE-THE-POOH

IF YOU HAVE not been feeling very 'how' for a while, the chances are you need a holiday. You take your car to the garage for regular services, have your boiler and your burglar alarm serviced (don't you?), so why not put your mind and body in for regular pit stops?

Holidays are hugely beneficial for putting you back together again, but in today's stressed work environment some people do not take their full holiday entitlement. Maybe they fear being dispensable, or they feel guilty about overloading over-stretched colleagues, or they can't face doing all the work they need to do beforehand to free themselves up for a holiday. Whatever the reason, it is not valid enough to cancel your holiday! Without regular holidays you remain exhausted and stressed and you will not be a long-term high performer. You will also have more time off sick.

To benefit from a holiday it needs to be at least two consecutive weeks long and during that time you should not keep in contact with work or worry about what is happening there. Of course if you can't get away for two weeks, take whatever time you can. To reduce any problems about going away, make a list as far in advance as possible of everything you would normally do if you were not on holiday and then delegate (with agreement from your boss and colleagues), reschedule, or drop the things on the list. But do not reschedule your holiday.

You also need to be careful to choose the right holiday. You will not enjoy it if it is the wrong holiday for you and anyone else you might be travelling with. If other people are involved, discuss beforehand what you all want to do. There's no point in taking an adventure holiday or trying a

new destination if even one of the party finds new experiences traumatic. Make sure the climate is OK for everyone and don't go somewhere that bores you – you'll spend more time drinking alcohol if you have nothing to do. Conversely, a hectic schedule in which every minute is filled with activities and sightseeing is not really a holiday. Don't be afraid to relax – it's fun.

It was going to be one of Rabbit's busy days. As soon as he woke up he felt important, as if everything depended upon him. It was just the day for Organizing Something, or for Writing a Notice Signed Rabbit, or for Seeing What Everybody Else Thought About It . . . It was a Captainish sort of day . . .

THE HOUSE AT POOH CORNER

'IF YOU WANT something done, ask a busy person,' goes the adage. In some instances that may work, but what if you are that busy person?

People who frantically fill their days with activities or take on rather more commitments than they have time for may feel very important and as if Everything Depends on Them. But are they and does it? Well, it may do, and of course some people are genuinely altruistic and do it without feeling at all important. Others do it because they lack self-esteem and feel this makes them Needed. But at what price? The danger of an overly busy mind, and an overly committed diary, is that it is virtually inevitable that you will make more mistakes and that sooner or later it will catch up with you and you will become exhausted. You might also resent the time you spend on others,

particularly if you feel taken for granted. Doing something in a resentful way is unattractive to you and the people who witness you doing it. So perhaps it is time to examine why you are doing so much.

It is possible that you are not the only capable person in your vicinity and that others could and should share the load. It could be that you are using all these activities as a displacement technique so that you do not have time to stop and think about something that is really bothering you, perhaps a fundamental issue in your life that would leave you happier if it were resolved. Is it time you made a commitment to yourself to stop taking on any more responsibilities or give some up?

However, not everyone can let their responsibilities go. It may be that you would love to but it is just not possible

– elderly parents, children, people with disabilities all need caring for and there may be no one else to do it, in which case, the last thing you want to do is feel guilty about having to be so busy. But it is vital to take some breaks – and we all feel better for counting our blessings, even when they may be (temporarily) in short supply.

Winnie-the-Pooh read the two notices very carefully, first from left to right, and afterwards, in case he had missed some of it, from right to left.

WINNIE-THE-POOH

HOW MANY TIMES have you been caught out by not reading the small print? Have you fallen for tricks such as 'Win a luxury home!' in today's *Daily Tittle Tattle,* only to find, when you have bought the paper and read the small print, that you need to buy the paper for the next twenty-eight consecutive days to collect the coupons to enter the draw . . . ? Hrrumph! There are more serious instances too – taking out loans, buying insurance for your home or car, making – and checking – your will. All these things need to be done with care and although it is boring (unless you like that kind of attention to tedious detail), it will pay in the long run. Next time you are made an offer you can't refuse or one that sounds too good to be true, first sleep on it, then apply a little healthy scepticism to your response, and finally check the facts before you sign an agreement. And before you do sign, check that there is a period of time, usually twenty-eight days, during which you can change your mind. Involve an independent expert if a lot of money or risk is involved because you need to be sure who is ultimately liable in any enterprise. Then, after signing, look at it again a week later, reading it from back to front, if necessary, just like Pooh.

Nobody seemed to know where they came from, but there they were in the Forest: Kanga and Baby Roo. When Pooh asked Christopher Robin, 'How did they come here?' Christopher Robin said, 'In the Usual Way, if you know what I mean, Pooh,' and Pooh, who didn't, said 'Oh!' Then he nodded his head twice and said, 'In the Usual Way. Ah!'

WINNIE-THE-POOH

KNOWING POOH TO be a Bear with a Pleasing Manner but a Positively Startling Lack of Brain, that is perhaps a predictable reaction. Poor Pooh stays in his confused state, like many of us, because he – and we – do not know how to probe any deeper. But if we are to relieve the foggy uncertainty in our minds and find out what we really want to know, then we have to be tenacious and persistent. It may be that the people who surround us do not have the answers we need, in which case we need to look further afield. So whether you are trying to find out the route of a proposed new road near your home, the name of your new neighbour or the Origins of Man, be prepared to do some research to unearth the facts. However, try not to go into information overload. You will need to limit the amount of research you do and be very discriminating. When you are offered an explanation, check the source of the information to see if it is authoritative, particularly if you are surfing the Internet for information or assistance. Don't just accept the assurances of others who may not themselves be in possession of all the facts.

It was a fine spring morning in the Forest as he started out. Little soft clouds played happily in a blue sky, skipping from time to time in front of the sun as if they had come to put it out, and then sliding away suddenly so that the next might have his turn. Through them and between them the sun shone bravely; and a copse which has worn its firs all the year round seemed old and dowdy now beside the new green lace which the beeches had put on so prettily. Through copse and spinney marched Bear; down open slopes of gorse and heather, over rocky beds of streams, up steep bands of sandstone into the heather again; and so at last, tired and hungry, to the Hundred Acre Wood.

WINNIE-THE-POOH

DOESN'T THAT DESCRIPTION take you right to the heart of the matter? Put a Gone to Lunch (Bisy Backson) notice on your door and take a walk in the Forest, bathe yourself in the light and smell of the warm pine trees, listen to the birds and catch the fragrant breeze.

If you live and work in a busy city or town, or commute long distances, an escape during your busy day to an oasis (park, garden, library, church) is oh-so-therapeutic. Of course, when you have more time you could go to the Hundred Acre Wood or walk in a real forest or visit a spa with hot springs, whether it is for a week or just a morning. You could make a retreat, either spiritual or pampering, of one of your annual holidays. At the weekend, find a relatively local place where you can walk or be quiet. It may be a bus, train or car journey away, but tranquillity in nature is worth seeking out. It is important to find time to enjoy the fruits of your hard work and escape from your busy world to an enchanted forest.

'Hallo, everybody,' said Christopher Robin – 'Hallo, Pooh.'
They all said 'Hallo,' and felt awkward and unhappy suddenly, because it was a sort of good-bye they were saying, and they didn't want to think about it. So they stood around, and waited for somebody else to speak, and they nudged each and, and said, 'Go on.'

THE HOUSE AT POOH CORNER

SAYING GOODBYE CAN be awkward and difficult; often the right words seem to evade you. Goodbyes are less frequently required than goodnights but each parting should be on good terms. You will sleep more easily if you do not carry daytime annoyances to bed with you – like anger and resentment, bad feelings are not good bedfellows. They tend to keep you awake all night with their Tiggerish 'Worraworraworraworraworra' buzzing away in your mind, nagging and goading you to renew the hostility you feel towards your enemy every time you roll over and punch the pillow.

Going to bed on good terms has its selfish side because it is definitely you who is going to suffer if you don't make peace, which is not to say you have to forgive and forget even if the other person is in the wrong. It means Happy Conflicts, finding amicable solutions to problems and differences within the family, or at least starting negotiations well before you go to bed.

So the next time you have had an argument or there's an atmosphere, offer to make the other person a cup of tea or cocoa before retiring for the night. Then you will sleep as soundly as Pooh.

'Getting Tigger down,' *said Eeyore, 'and* Not hurting anybody. *Keep those two ideas in your head, Piglet, and you'll be all right.'*

THE HOUSE AT POOH CORNER

TIGGER'S IMPETUOSITY MAY have led him to climb too high up the tree on his incautious outing with Roo but his risk-taking behaviour might make him a high-flyer in the business world, whereas Eeyore would never take unnecessary risks or do anything impetuous or incautious. He is always careful to look after himself, to his detriment ironically, as his social life and laughter fund are running low. However, he has made an astute observation about the dilemma facing those trying to get Tigger down from the tree, and it is one that can be applied to most tasks: do the best you can within an acceptable range of risk. At work, you can translate this into 'Don't put your health and psychological well-being in jeopardy for the sake of getting the job done.'

This applies in all other areas of life too, from personal finance to activity holidays. For example, a boss who is habitually unfair and unreasonable is bad for your health and can send your blood pressure soaring, which could in the long term increase your risk of heart disease or stroke. If you are the boss, consider the health of your employees struggling to meet another deadline.

We need to keep a sense of perspective about the tasks we tackle. There is an acceptable (and enjoyable) level of risk and there is an intolerable element of risk. Keep those two in balance and you'll be all right, as Eeyore says.

. . . Christopher Robin said: 'What do you like doing best in the world, Pooh?'

'Well,' said Pooh, 'what I like best – ' and then he had to stop and think. Because although Eating Honey was a very good thing to do, there was a moment just before you began to eat it which was better than when you were, but he didn't know what it was called. And then he thought that being with Christopher Robin was a very good thing to do, and having Piglet near was a very friendly thing to have; and so, when he had thought it all out, he said, 'What I like best in the whole world is Me and Piglet going to see You, and You saying "What about a little something?" and Me saying, "Well, I shouldn't mind a little something, should you, Piglet," and it being a hummy sort of day outside, and birds singing.'

THE HOUSE AT POOH CORNER

AAH, WHAT BLISS! Everyone will have a different Perfect Day, but the thing that all will have in common is that the activity – or lack of it – will be something they will have determined themselves. So much of what we do in life is determined by others that we need to make time for what we like doing most of all. While we cannot do everything we want, when we want, we can try to focus our efforts on the role(s) we enjoy most and perform best. Often that is where we make a difference, such as making life more pleasant for partners, children and friends, and more pleasant for those in our neighbourhood.

The reward is a greater feeling of control over our lives and a better sense of mental and physical well-being. When you know you have time for pursuing your interests and things that are a pleasure to you, then you will be happier to do the tasks assigned by others on the days that are not entirely your own. And even on the days that do not feel like your own you can add enjoyment by finding time for a well-made cup of coffee, or wearing a flower in your lapel. Like many of us, Pooh enjoys most the company of food – and friends! But there are many other ways we can satisfy our senses.

Well, he was humming this hum to himself, and walking gaily along . . . when suddenly he came to a sandy bank, and in the bank was a large hole. 'Aha!' said Pooh. (Rum-tum-tiddle-um-tum.) *'If I know anything about anything, that hole means Rabbit,'* he said, *'and Rabbit means Company,'* he said, *'and Company means Food and Listening-to-Me Humming and such like . . .'*

WINNIE-THE-POOH

POOH IS A sociable bear. He has a big network of friends. He is interested in their welfare and they in his. He doesn't have Rabbit's large number of relatives, but his social network is more effective than Rabbit's. And that means a lot, because the bigger your social network, the longer, happier and healthier your life is likely to be. So pop back to the Hundred Acre Wood as frequently as you can to enjoy the company of Pooh and Piglet and all the others.

There is something else available to you in the Hundred Acre Wood – peace and a comfortable solitude in which you can think. Pooh is a Great Thinker. The combination of freedom of thought and companionship allows him to be

at ease with himself and the others. Recognising that our thoughts influence hugely whether we feel positive or negative is a significant discovery.

Pooh also lets go of negative thoughts. He acknowledges them (some can, some can't) then quite rightly leaves it at that. He does not dwell on them and we can learn a lot from that. If we try to think more positively, like Pooh, we will feel a lot better about ourselves and enjoy better relationships with others.

Finding space for thought in a place where you can also find friendship is very valuable. This unique combination makes the Hundred Acre Wood a very special place, and with Pooh always there it becomes a unique place too in which friendship, sharing and caring, for yourself and others, are the Most Important Things.

Which they are.

'Is that the end of the story?' asked Christopher Robin.
'That's the end of that one. There are others.'
'About Pooh and Me?'
'And Piglet and Rabbit and all of you. Don't you remember?'
'I do remember, and then when I try to remember, I forget.'

WINNIE-THE-POOH

LIKE MOST PEOPLE there are times when you think, or even worry, that your memory isn't as sharp as it used to be – you can't put names to faces and forget facts you've known since schooldays, or even forget appointments. Naturally you wonder how normal this is, especially when, as Christopher Robin describes above, the more you try to remember the less able you seem to be to recall. Unless you are really getting on your memory loss is probably more likely to be due to the stress of trying to juggle too many things, sleep problems or lack of stimulation than it is to any underlying conditions such as premature dementia. (Well, that's a relief.)

To improve things, you need to do more 'cognitive' (mental or mind-stretching) activities. Find a child with whom to play 'My Grandmother Went to Market' (in which you memorise an increasingly long list of items bought by the grandmother), or invest in a good book of brainteasers, crosswords and puzzles, or learn another language, – a brilliant device for regenerating and building new connections in the brain.

Take more exercise to jog those neurons into activity and eat five portions of fresh fruit and vegetables daily for their antioxidant Vitamin C: memory tests on older people show the highest scores among people with the highest intakes of fruits and vegetables. Don't watch too much television; while it's possible for television to be intellectually stimulating, the reality is that most of the time you're watching TV you are in a catatonic state: you are not learning anything, and it's learning and physical activity that keep the brain active. So switch off the TV, get up off the couch and be more active.